THE

MORAL

OF THE

STORY

Also by the Author

Becoming Friends
Worship, Justice, and the
Practice of Christian Friendship

Friendship and Moral Life

The Primacy of Love
An Introduction to the Ethics
of Thomas Aquinas

Friends of God
Virtues and Gifts in Aquinas

Morality
A Course on Catholic Living

THE

MORAL

OF THE

STORY

Learning from Literature about
HUMAN AND DIVINE LOVE

PAUL J. WADELL

A Herder & Herder Book
The Crossroad Publishing Company
New York

The Crossroad Publishing Company
481 Eighth Avenue, New York, NY 10001

Printed in the United States of America

Library of Congress Cataloging-in-Publication Data
Wadell, Paul J.
    The moral of the story : learning from literature about human and divine love / Paul J. Wadell.
        p.   cm.
    "A Herder & Herder book."
    Includes bibliographical references.
    ISBN 0-8245-1980-9 (alk. paper)
    1. American fiction – 20th century – History and criticism.
2. Christian fiction, American – History and criticism. 3. Didactic fiction, American – History and criticism. 4. Percy, Walker, 1916– . Second coming. 5. Gordon, Mary, 1949– . Final payments. 6. Tyler, Anne. Saint maybe. 7. Greene, Graham, 1904– . Heart of the matter. 8. Fugard, Athol. My children! My Africa! 9. Christian ethics in literature.   I. Title.
PS374.C48W33 2002
813′.5093823 – dc21
                                        2002011119

1   2   3   4   5   6   7   8   9   10   08   07   06   05   04   03   02

To Four Whose Stories Have Blessed Me

James DeManuele, C.P.
Germain Legere, C.P.
Sebastian MacDonald, C.P.
Kenneth O'Malley, C.P.

CONTENTS

INTRODUCTION

I N A PAST LIFE I used to be an English major. Out of an array of possible college majors, I chose English for no other reason than I liked to read novels. But this created a problem when graduate studies in theology led to teaching theology: With so many books to read in theology, how could I sneak time with a novel? Would novel reading be restricted to vacations and time spent on airplanes? Fortunately my friend Edward Beck came to the rescue. One day when driving to Midway Airport in Chicago, I shared with him my frustration. His solution was swift and nifty: why not teach a class exploring theological and moral themes in literature?

His suggestion made sense because ever since high school when some very gifted teachers opened up the world of great literature to us, I have been convinced that the best theology, the best philosophy, and the best psychology can be found in the best literature. Where better to encounter the transformative power of Christ's death and resurrection than in the story of Raskolnikov's fall and regeneration in Dostoyevsky's *Crime and Punishment*? Where better to view the sad results of a life bewitched by the fantasies of wealth than in F. Scott Fitzgerald's beautiful and poignant novel *The Great Gatsby*?

Literature is a powerful source of moral education because it works on our hearts as well as our minds. The power of a good story is that it draws us into its world. We learn from observing how the characters in a novel or play react to different people and different situations. We watch as they deal with challenges and difficult choices in their lives. We see their character being formed by how they respond to suffering as well as success. We learn whose behavior we should imitate and whose behavior we should shun. And since great literature is a blend of noble ideas as well as noble emotions, it forms and shapes our affections so that we sympathize with the suffering, protest with the oppressed, and honor the faithful. Literature has the power to challenge us and to change us. It can make us see the world, as well as ourselves, differently. It expands our horizons, challenges our assumptions, and sometimes, like the short stories of Flannery O'Connor, turns everything upside down. Is it too much to say good literature can make us better?

This book is neither a theology text nor a book of literary criticism; rather, it is a moral and theological reflection on some of the fundamental issues, questions, and challenges facing human beings, but a reflection pursued in dialogue with literary works that wrestle with those same themes and questions. The book is designed for people who may never pick up a text in either theology or ethics, but who often find themselves thinking about the nature and existence of God; the problem of evil and how easy it is to live wayward lives; the sobering and inescapable reality of suffering, and how hard it is to reconcile suffering with a God who is supposed to be absolute love; the crippling fact of injustice and the kind of moral imagination needed to re-envision the world in hope; the deep need for forgiveness, but how difficult it is to understand what forgiveness is and demands; or, simply, when immersed in sadness to discover what might be our reasons for joy.

Chapter 1 focuses on the most fundamental and enduring moral obligation of our lives: the call to choose life over death each day. The heart of the Christian gospel is that life is more powerful than death, and that life and love, not death, finally triumph. But sometimes it is hard to believe this truth, much less *live this truth,* not only because of the violence and viciousness that keep breaking out among us, but also because we fail to see how so many things we pursue in life are little more than death disguised. And so we shut ourselves up in tombs, hardly realizing we can never find life there and seldom considering what life would look like outside of the tomb. But God wants life, freedom, and love for us, not death-in-life and despair. God wants us to break free from the tombs of our lives, not reinforce them. God wants us to triumph over the powers of death, not be seduced by them. How then do we break free from the tombs of our lives? How do we live in hope? How can we live in the power of Easter *today?* These are questions chapter 1 will explore.

Many works of literature would aid us in reflecting on these questions. In chapter 1 I explore them in conversation with Walker Percy's novel *The Second Coming*, the story of Will Barrett, a man trapped in a despair so ordinary that he hardly thinks anything is amiss. But eventually disenchantment surfaces, and Will Barrett begins his journey back to hope and life through the grace of an unexpected love. At the end of chapter 1, as well as the other chapters, I suggest other novels and plays, and some works of nonfiction, that could also be helpful for anyone who might want to consider these questions further.

Chapter 2 probes two inseparable mysteries: the mystery of human waywardness and the mystery of God's inexhaustible love. It analyzes both a theological understanding of what it means to be human and a theology of God that is rich in hope and reassurance, but also somewhat unnerving because it teaches that God's power consists not in a capacity to alleviate human suffering and defeat, but to enter into them redemptively; in other words, God's power is compassionate love.

Graham Greene's *The Heart of the Matter* is the book I chose for considering these questions. It is a novel which emphatically reminds us that we are a long way from Eden. Greene's characters are a fallen people in a fallen world, a shipwrecked bunch for whom the world is more a place of exile than home. Through the story of Scobie, the major character in *The Heart of the Matter*, Greene unmasks the brokenness and corruption that beat at the heart of every human being and shatters our illusions of innocence. This does not mean redemptive possibilities are beyond us, but if they exist they are surely sign of the resolute goodness of a God whose love stops at nothing to save us, and not the achievements of our own virtue. Is this the "heart of the matter," the belief that despite our faults and our failings there lives a God of merciful compassion who will stop at nothing to reach us? And if this is true, is anyone ever beyond hope? Out of love's reach?

Everyone knows human beings must learn how to love. And everyone knows Christianity is about learning how to love. But how should human beings love? The gospels teach that faithful imitators of Jesus ought to love everybody, but should we (and can we) love everyone in exactly the same way? Should we love some more than others? Or some not at all? These are questions raised in Mary Gordon's *Final Payments*, the novel studied in chapter 3. It is the story of Isabel Moore, a woman whose beliefs about love almost prove deadly. Can we pay too great a price for love? Is the best love always the most demanding? Love is a matter of heartfelt devotion, but some devotions of the heart are more destructive than graced. We all know people whose faithful love killed their spirits, people whose devotion was more annihilating than life-giving. Jesus calls us to love our enemies, but what do we do when a loved one becomes our enemy? We cannot stop loving them, but shouldn't the way we love them change? Love is such a sticky subject. We cannot live without it, but we can spend a lifetime trying to figure it out. In *Final Payments* Mary Gordon suggests we need to learn the meaning of love but also *the limits* of love. Even if we are called to love like God, God can love in ways we cannot. But how do we keep this fact from placing unjustified restrictions on our love? How do we resist narrowing our love to only those "neighbors" we like? We will wrestle with these questions in chapter 3 as we explore the nature, meaning, and limits of love.

Is the world mastered by injustice? It can seem so when each year millions of lives are deemed expendable so that some can prosper with far more than they ever deserve. Injustice is so deeply embedded in the institutions, structures, and practices of our world that we can hardly imagine what the world would be like without it. We take for granted that some will have power and others will not. It seems unavoidable — almost perfectly natural — that some will be scandalously wealthy and others will be scandalously poor. The tyranny of injustice has never been broken, so why would we expect things to be different today? But only the comfortable can afford to postpone justice. Those whose lives are pulverized by the greed, materialism, selfishness, and sheer indifference of the prosperous know justice cannot be delayed because injustice kills.

Chapter 4 turns to these questions of justice, exploring the meaning and nature of justice, the vicious and destructive powers of injustice, and how injustice can be overcome and justice restored. It probes these matters through Athol Fugard's play *My Children! My Africa!*, a work that focuses on the injustice spawned by the demonic system of apartheid in South Africa. However, although *My Children! My Africa!* takes place in a society that might seem far different from our own, the play has a message for all of us because the obligations of justice are ignored worldwide everyday. Fugard prompts us to ask whether the way we live each day brings harm to others somewhere else in the world. Do our patterns of consumption, our use of resources, or our accumulation of wealth make it hard for others to live at all? Does the comfort I enjoy today leave somebody else desolate? These questions disturb us and they should. Injustice is a sin that calls for a conversion in our attitudes, our expectations, our habits and practices, and our moral vision; however, it also calls for a radical transformation in the politics and economics of our world. Justice is not a lifestyle option; it is the most fundamental and inescapable moral obligation we have toward others. Chapter 4 reflects on the meaning of justice, the scourge of injustice, and the kind of moral imagination needed if injustice is to be overcome and justice restored.

The fifth and final chapter centers on forgiveness. None of us can get through life without forgiving and being forgiven, but we live in a world that easily misunderstands what real forgiveness is. We want forgiveness to be quick, easy, neat, and not very demanding. But such cheap forgiveness never works, first because it is not truthful, and second because it is more cosmetic than real. There is nothing more powerful than real forgiveness because real forgiveness heals, restores, and renews; indeed, real forgiveness is so innovative and creative that it can redeem the past in hope.

But this happens only when we grasp that forgiveness is more than a single act; indeed, it is the call to live a wholly new way of life, a forgiven and forgiving way of life. This is the message of Anne Tyler's wonderful novel *Saint Maybe*, the book we will work from in chapter 5. *Saint Maybe* is the story of Ian Bedloe, a good-hearted young man whose life was upended by something he deeply regretted but could not undo. Ian has to find a way to move beyond something that makes him feel terribly guilty and keeps him from knowing either freedom or peace. He has to learn how to redeem what he cannot erase.

Ian Bedloe is no different from the rest of us. Forgiveness is indispensable for any person's life because eventually our lives break down through hurts, misunderstandings, disappointments, terrible betrayals, or unspeakable evil. None of us moves through life without wounding others or being wounded ourselves. No one, however fortunate, avoids the kind of suffering and heartbreak that leaves us wondering, "How does life go on?"

Christianity is all about second chances and new beginnings; indeed, if Christians know anything they should know what it means to be forgiven and to forgive. But they should also know that forgiveness, *precisely because it is a gift*, is an invitation to live differently. Forgiveness fascinates because everyone needs it and most of us struggle in giving it. In chapter 5 we will investigate the power and purpose of forgiveness, asking not only what does forgiveness tell us about ourselves, but also what does forgiveness tell us about God? In exploring these matters we shall learn that the freest, and perhaps the most joyous person, is the grateful person, and the person of true gratitude is not the person for whom all has gone well, but the person who lives a forgiven and forgiving life in hope.

CHAPTER ONE

BEGINNING
THE MORAL ADVENTURE

Choosing Life over Death Each Day

D EATH SEEMS TO BE WINNING. That's a shocking statement but, after the terrible events of September 11, not an unreasonable one. Who of us can ever erase from our memories those wrenching images of planes being flown into the World Trade Center in New York and the Pentagon in Washington, D.C.? That day we were not only confronted with horrible, unthinkable evil, but perhaps also wondered if the forces of evil were indeed stronger than the powers for good.

We live in a world where oftentimes death does seem stronger than life. Terrorist bombs blow planes out of the sky and routinely bring death in the Middle East. Catholics and Protestants find new ways to bloody one another in Northern Ireland, and rival ethnic groups, drunk on the toxins of hate, kill with gleeful abandon in Africa and Yugoslavia.

Closer to home, we are no longer surprised when we hear of disgruntled workers exploding in rage and resentment, bidding farewell to life in one grand gesture of self-righteousness as they kill everyone around them before putting a bullet to themselves. Similarly, murder, then suicide, can seem an almost standard way for jilted lovers to have the last word with those who have rejected them. Are we any longer surprised to read of ex-husbands or ex-wives who, with some twisted sense of justice, think the only way to even the score is by destroying everyone they once claimed most to love?

Even more unsettling, death has seduced the disturbed and disillusioned among our young, as adolescents on the threshold of life celebrate their disenchantment by killing their peers before destroying themselves. Paducah, Kentucky; Jonesboro, Arkansas; Springfield, Oregon; Edinboro, Pennsylvania; Pearl, Mississippi; and Littleton, Colorado: the names ring out as stops on an itinerary of hopelessness we have little idea how to derail. What frightens us is not only the fact that these shootings have happened, but that we have such little confidence the bloody tragedies will not happen again. This is a nightmare that just keeps unfolding.

Morality is a matter of choosing life over death *each day,* but in our strange and frightening world it is easy to believe that death is more powerful than life. Death wins every time hatred triumphs over love. It wins every time vengeance and vindictiveness triumph over forgiveness and reconciliation. It wins when sadness makes a stranger of joy and despair makes hope a fanciful dream. Death smiles when cruelty abounds, when truthfulness and integrity are derided, and when faithfulness is considered quaint. And death especially rejoices when justice is forgotten, when the poor and the weak are deemed expendable, and when those who are different are viewed not as blessings but as threats.

Somewhere the demons are laughing. There is something diabolical about any situation in which death is sovereign. There is something sadly perverse about people who surrender to death and everything death-dealing because they secretly believe death is more powerful than life, and death, not life, is the truth of things. That is how it can seem in a world where a hopeful life is so easily misplaced. Death can be stealing our life away and we hardly know it because we have forgotten what it really means to live. Joy, peace, hope, and satisfaction have for so long been absent from our lives that we have no idea death has chained our spirits in despair.

The great cosmic lie exposed once and for all by the resurrection is that death rules life. But that lie is an enticing seduction because there is something in our own broken spirits and in our increasingly broken world that secretly worships the lie and lets it capture our hearts. Then the chains of death broken by Christ's resurrection are forged together again and ensnare another victim. Held tight in the bondage of darkness and death, we spend our days in cozy tombs as Easter passes us by. No wonder the demons are laughing.

But what if there is another way? What would life look like *outside of the tomb?* What would it mean to live the gospel message that life is stronger than death and light more powerful than all the darkness around us? These questions go to the heart of the moral life; indeed, how we answer them determines whether our own moral journey will be traveled in hope or despair. In this opening chapter I want to reflect on the moral life as the ongoing challenge to choose life over death each day, and to examine this idea in conversation with Walker Percy's novel *The Second Coming.*[1]

It is the story of Will Barrett, a man who is fabulously wealthy and the envy of all, but who, despite what everyone takes to be the best possible life, walks around with a pistol in his pocket because he is thinking of putting a bullet in his brain. Death hovers over this novel because Barrett has yet to name the demons with which he must wrestle if he is ever to break free and to live. But *The Second Coming* is also an Easter story, a saga of paschal restoration, not only because it plots the path of a man born again through love, but also because it steadfastly insists the most terrible sin we can commit against ourselves or others is to let death in any of its forms prevail.

Our most basic moral task is to choose life; however, as the story of Will Barrett attests, oftentimes we do not understand what it means for us to choose life unless we first recognize all the things we pursue that are little more than death disguised. At the heart of the Christian life, and indeed the gospels, beats the conviction that a God who is love and freedom and life wants love, freedom, and life for us. But we must want these for ourselves, and others as well, and devote ourselves to securing them. Anyone who understands the gift of life is determined to resist the seductions of death.

But it is never easy, and *The Second Coming* shows us why. The saga of Will Barrett is the story of a man who moves from the grip of death to the joy of life through love. But his resurrection comes slowly and with great difficulty precisely because the forces of death are so strong. The same is true for us. What makes *The Second Coming* such a riveting moral tale is that it goes to the heart of the drama of every human life. How do we live in hope? How do we break out of the tombs of our lives? How, despite all the difficulties and setbacks of life, do we live in the power of Easter joy? In this chapter, we shall explore the healing and restoration of Will Barrett by considering (1) why it is that the path to new life often begins in disenchantment; (2) why new life demands that we confront the powers of darkness and death in ourselves and in our world; and (3) why the only power we have over darkness and death is love. In the process we shall discover why Easter is not just a feast, but a gracious and hopeful way of life we are called to embrace and embody.

Why the Path to New Life
Often Begins in Disenchantment

Sometimes the most momentous changes of our lives are born from disenchantment. That is how it is with Will Barrett. We get a clue of this in the opening line of the novel: "The first sign that something had gone wrong manifested itself while he was playing golf."[2] That sentence propels the book. Something has gone wrong in Will Barrett's life, but he is not sure why. While others "appear to live normally, work as usual, play golf, tell jokes, argue politics,"[3] Barrett has "been feeling depressed without knowing why,"[4] a misfit in a world where everyone else seems to belong. While others live seemingly happy, untroubled lives, he grows distant not only from them, but also from himself. Alienation pervades him so that what makes sense to everyone else, for him grows "more senseless and farcical with each passing day."[5]

The starting point for many of Walker Percy's novels is the major characters' conviction that something has gone wrong with them and their world, but hardly anyone else notices. There is a crisis few recognize because at first glance all seems to be well. But the problem with first glances is they don't show us enough; they are not adequately revealing. At first glance, Will Barrett should be amazingly happy because he has everything everyone else wants. He is wealthy, liked, and has all the freedom money can buy; in fact, his friends envy the life that now leaves him restless and confused. They presume his life is trouble free, but the truth is every day Will Barrett imagines escaping his life by blowing out his brains. In what everyone assumes is the best of all possible lives, Will Barrett is miserable. Contemplating his life he concludes, "This is not for me."[6]

Although Barrett cannot yet see it, that confession of disenchantment is the seed for a new beginning. We will not leave one kind of life to search for something better unless we feel something is seriously amiss with the life we have been living. Discontent makes us question; so do boredom, restlessness, depression, and the unsuppressible conviction that as good as our life seems to be, something important is missing. Disenchantment is a powerful source for moral and spiritual change because it gives us the energy we need to break free from destructive habits and practices, from long accepted but deadening customs, and from mesmerizing but empty ideologies in order to search for something more. Realizing we are not satisfied with the life we have made our own, even if our friends, our family, our churches, or our society says such a life should content us, can give us the courage we need to imagine more hopeful possibilities. This is what happens to Barrett. He has what everyone says he should want but he is not happy, and that dissatisfaction is enough to prompt him to look for something new and something better. It is his rejection of a deadening way of life that begins his search for a gracious and hopeful way of life.

His sense that there must be something more, his growing certainty that beautiful homes, lots of money, status, and prestige cannot be the truth of things frees Will Barrett to break with the conventional and undertake the quest for a deeper, more lasting happiness and a genuinely humanizing life. In fact, it is his growing suspicion that what his friends take to be the good life is not life at all but only *death disguised*, that throws Barrett into panic and has him in anxious pursuit of something hopeful and life-giving. If wealth, comfort, and pleasure do not constitute true life, what does?

Such suspicion, although initially disconcerting, is a saving grace. Suspicion feeds on dissatisfaction and can lead to new understanding and new ways of seeing and thinking and living. Suspicion leads to hope when it no longer allows us to be controlled by answers which increasingly make no sense to us and by customs and practices which leave us sad and unfree. Suspicion and discontent can be life-giving and liberating graces because they alert us to the danger of accepting too uncritically what others tell us we need and, therefore, should care for and love. Armed with suspicion and disenchantment, we can, like Will Barrett, detect the emptiness in so many of the ideologies of our culture and its institutions, and then find others with whom to create something better.

Suspicion and discontent are blessings when they break the hold the world has on us and empower us to strike out for something new. We need to see the vacuity of much of modern life if we are to find the courage necessary to seek something new and try something better. The problem for most of us, however, is that we are not suspicious enough; rather, we are far too enchanted with the way things are, so entranced with the prevailing arrangements of life that it never dawns on us that life could be other, and better, than it is.

The grace of disenchantment is precisely its ability to make us question what we are constantly encouraged to accept. It is essential for the moral life because if we foster the wrong kinds of attachments or nurture the wrong kinds of loves, we shall grow in all the wrong ways. Human beings are creatures of devotion — we love to give our hearts away — but misplaced devotions always bottom out in despair. We need to choose our attachments wisely because we become morally and spiritually malformed through wayward loves, whether they be for money, possessions, pleasure, or guns. Greed, consumerism, hedonism, power, and violence are the crippling idols of our age. Loving them not only makes us superficial; it also makes us dangerous because such loves are morally and spiritually disfiguring. We become what we love, taking on the form of our most perduring attachments. If such love be for God, goodness, justice, and peace we shall find life. It is no accident that Jesus *commanded us to love* God and neighbor wholeheartedly. In that command lies the path to freedom and life because wholehearted love for anything else ineluctably leads to death.

But it is easy to stroll down paths of death; for many people it is where they spend most of their lives. In *The Second Coming* Will Barrett is not the only one in trouble. Something is wrong with the others as well, but they are too enchanted with the conventional to perceive it. They think they are enjoying the best of all possible worlds because they lack the vision — the moral imagination really — to see their lives clearly. Locked in the fantasies of consumerism and materialism, they

do not realize how hollow and hopeless their lives really are. They
need to be disenchanted in order to be free, but only Barrett is trou-
bled enough to grasp what they miss. He knows what they embrace
as fulfilling is actually stunting. He realizes what they celebrate as the
good life is really more death-in-life. Barrett sees them not as thriving
and prosperous and happy, but as anesthesized by the ever changing
amusements that constitute contemporary life. It is Barrett the misfit, Barrett the strange, who sees them better than they see themselves.
This weird man who falls down on golf courses, reminisces about long-
lost loves, is bored with his wealth, and carries a pistol in his pocket
is a stranger to them and perhaps even a stranger to himself. But he
sees better than they do, and he knows they are in trouble. Like a
prophet scanning the horizon, Barrett gives this unsettling assessment
of himself and his friends:

> As for Will Barrett, as for people nowadays — they were never
> a hundred percent themselves.... More likely they were forty-
> seven percent themselves.... All too often these days they were
> two percent themselves, specters who hardly occupied a place
> at all....
>
> There was his diagnosis, then. A person nowadays is two per-
> cent himself. And to arrive at a diagnosis is already to have
> anticipated the cure: how to restore the ninety-eight percent?[7]

How to restore the missing ninety-eight percent? This is the question guiding *The Second Coming*, but it is also a question that ought to
guide our lives. If something about how we live robs us of life, then we
need to find the thief. If we live, like Will Barrett, with the unsettling
awareness that something crucial to our life is missing, we ought to care
enough about ourselves (and others) to find out what it is. Or if we
find ourselves unhappy, depressed, and flirting with despair we should
battle those demons, not surrender to them. Our fundamental moral
obligation is always to choose life. But oftentimes we cannot choose
life unless we first diagnose what is bringing us death. The tombs of
our lives can be many: destructive relationships, painful memories that
have not healed, harmful habits we have not been able to break, attachments that diminish. No life escapes such tombs, but the worst
thing to do is to settle down in those tombs and allow them to become

our home. We should never settle for stunted, diminished lives either for ourselves or for others. To do so is a sin against the God who made us, a sin against ourselves, and a sin against all those whom our life is meant to bless.

Chapter 1 of *The Second Coming* ends with Will Barrett wondering who the enemy is. If everyone seems diminished and depressed, there must be an enemy at work. Who is the enemy depriving Barrett and others of life? With what must they contend if they are to live? Percy's point is that something must be overcome — some demon wrestled with, some enemy vanquished — if the missing ninety-eight percent is to be restored. An abiding challenge of the moral life is to recognize and confront all the life-robbing forces in our world and in ourselves. To settle down with them, to affirm or nurture them, to grow complacent with them is to kiss death. It is the antithesis of Easter, a kind of cosmic blasphemy, because it completely violates the life God wants to be ours. Like Will Barrett, we need to be alert to the enemies of life. Most importantly, we should never grant them mastery. To believe they must prevail is the deadliest temptation. The central message of Christianity is that we are not to succumb to these life-robbing forces but, with God's help, overcome them.

Living beyond the Boundaries of the Conventional

Barrett will, but his path to regeneration takes an odd twist. It begins with a recently developed golf slice, a fortuitous quirk that has him moving from the fairways to the rough. An accomplished golfer, Barrett had always hit his drives straightaway; however, lately, to the dismay of his companions, he had been playing more and more out-of-bounds. "The slice, which had become worrisome lately, had gotten worse," Percy writes. "He had come to see it as an emblem of his life...." Barrett had been "banished from the pleasant licit fairways and the sunny irenic greens ... past the rough, past even the barbed wire fence, and into the dark fens and thickets and briars of out-of-bounds."[8]

The slice takes him outside his normal lifelines, leading him beyond the boundaries of his familiar world into the thickets of the unknown and unexplored. It is there Barrett will make his discovery. This pull out-of-bounds, this unexpected decentering, is actually a saving grace, proof that God's providence can be found anywhere in life, even in errant golf swings. Barrett must discover what is missing in his life; however, he can make that discovery only by being drawn beyond the parameters of his customary world. He cannot see what he needs to see if he remains in the familiar landscape of everyday life; rather, like the Israelites of old who find the Promised Land only by first risking the desert, Barrett's rebirth will come only when his ordinary world is first turned upside down.

Barrett needs to be renewed, but to achieve this transformation he must undertake a journey which will carry him far outside the world with which he is accustomed. And like the Israelites in Egypt, if he stays where he is he will never find life but only know the slavery of death-in-life. To live anew he must follow the promptings of grace even when they leave him in exile. If Barrett is again to find life and grace and hope in the world of the everyday, he must first leave that world for one that is uncharted and unknown. "Perhaps, he thought, even God will manifest himself when you are bent far enough out of your everyday lifeline."[9]

Meeting Someone Who Has Been in Exile and Is Coming Back

Eventually Barrett will encounter God, but he meets Allison Vaught first. Allison is the other major character of *The Second Coming* and when we meet her she is about to reconnect with life after having been exiled in a psychiatric hospital for three long years. When she first appears in the novel, Allison, having successfully plotted her escape from the hospital, walks around the streets of Linwood, North Carolina, a nearby town, trying to get her bearings in a world she hardly knows; she is an alien, a misfit in a world everyone else seems to understand. She describes herself as having "been away for a long time,"[10] and, Percy adds, "[s]he had felt like Rip Van Winkle coming down into town after a twenty-year nap."[11] Allison slipped away from the hospital after her electroshock treatment, "the beginning of the sixth (I think) course of electroconvulsive therapy, or ECT, known hereabouts as buzzing."[12] When she reenters the world she is not sure what year it is; in fact, because the electroshocks have shuffled her memory, she is not even sure of her name.

Allison returns to a world she had to flee in order to survive. The life everyone said was best for her was killing her. She was not sure if she was crazy, but everyone else found Allison odd, a straight-A student who had "flunked ordinary living."[13] But Allison could not help but wonder what was crazier: she or the rules for ordinary living? The question she kept asking herself was, "After you make straight A's, what do you do? How do you live?" Allison was a mystery to her parents because she refused to conform to what they believed would be best for her: "I didn't get married, I didn't get engaged, I don't even go steady. I didn't move on like I was supposed to."[14]

To protect herself, Allison retreated, pulling deep down inside herself where no one could touch her and she could not be hurt. She called this "going down to it, my white dwarf."[15] Allison felt safe there because it was the one place her life could be her own. Sitting in a closet, hidden away from all who thought they knew what was best for her, mumbling nonsense syllables because nothing made sense in her life anyway and nonsense was the one thing she could claim as her own, Allison collapsed in on herself, floating further and further out of the reach of her parents, her teachers, and the ordinary everyday world. As she explains, "My mother refused to let me fail. So I insisted."[16]

But Allison was not really failing; rather, she was drowning in a life that choked all hope and joy out of her. Life on her parents' terms was killing her, so she checked out of it and into a psychiatric hospital where, oddly enough, things seemed a little more sane. Like Will Barrett, Allison was disenchanted enough with what passed for a promising life to begin to believe there had to be something more. And, like Barrett, the only way she could discover what her life could be was by traveling far outside everything it had become. If Barrett must walk into the darkness of the rough to be resurrected, Allison had to go crazy. For both Will and Allison, disenchantment led to exile, but exile will eventually lead them to new awareness and to new hope. When Allison appears in the novel, she is like an infant taking its first feeble steps. She is awkward and groping — she hardly yet has her balance — but she is coming back to life.

Allison is a convalescent, a wounded warrior who is just starting her recovery. At the beginning of *The Second Coming* she is feeble and infirm, but at least she has broken free from the debilitating sickness of one kind of life and is searching for healing and hope and happiness in another kind of life. She is not yet fully well, but she is moving back to life, she is making a new start. In the language of Easter, the stone has been rolled back and she is taking her first steps outside of the tomb. While Will Barrett must yet die to life as he knows it, Allison, having made that passage, feels the exultation of a fresh new beginning. She still must travel far to break free from all that steals her life away, and it is clear that much pain and confusion await her, but her resurrection has begun. She has had her time in the tomb and is, however slowly, coming back to life. The three years in the hospital were a battle for her, and one that left her bruised and shaken, but new life is pouring into her. The long dark night is over for Allison and Easter is on its way. About her first day out of the hospital, Percy writes,

> Her body was sore. Her arms and legs hurt, one side of her jaw was swollen, her ribs felt as if she had taken a beating. But there was also the feeling that she was over the worst of it. Perhaps, she thought, it was like the pain one feels after being in a fight and winning. It was the kind of soreness the sun cures. The bench and her position on the bench had been arranged so that the morning sunlight hit the sore parts of her body. She felt like a snake stretched out on a rock in the sun, shedding its skin after a long hard winter.[17]

Why New Life Demands That We Confront the Powers of Darkness and Death

Unlike Allison, who is coming back to life, for Will Barrett the struggle is just beginning. What oppresses him is not, like Allison, the tyranny of other people's expectations, but a life that seems turned toward death, even ruled by death. Barrett is haunted by his father's secret love for death, his father's disabling conviction that death is the final truth of things, and death, not life, ultimately prevails. It is Will's perverse inheritance, the demon from which he must be freed. For more than thirty years he has been stalked by his father's obsession with death and his father's absolute assurance that Will would be just like him, not a lover of life but a victim of death-in-life: "You and I are the same.... You are like me," his father said to him. "We are two of a kind. I saw it last night.... You're one of us, I'm afraid. You already know too much."[18]

But Will is not yet fully aware of what his father says he knows. His life has been governed by an event he has struggled hard to suppress; however, suppressing it has not made it disappear, it has only strengthened its sovereignty over him. Only by naming and wrestling with this memory can Will be free. To pass from death-in-life to life he must reconnoiter with a memory living deep inside him that for more than thirty years has not only exerted a power over his life, but indeed has been the controlling center of his life, the point, however unconsciously, from which he has interpreted and responded to everything. His life is ruled by a long-ago event from which he has never recovered and does not now want to remember.

But remember it he must if he is ever to be healed, and so his path to recovery begins the day his body reconnects him to a memory. In typical Percy fashion, it happens when Will is playing golf and has sliced another shot out-of-bounds. He wanders into the rough looking for his ball and twists his arms in such a way that his muscles unlock a memory he thought was safely buried.

> Lifting the three-iron slowly and watching it all the while, once again he held it like a shotgun at rest, club head held high between his chest and arm, shaft resting across his forearm. Now, carefully, as if he were reenacting an event not quite remembered, as if he had forgotten something which his muscles and arms and hands might remember, he swung the shaft of the iron slowly to and fro like the barrel of a shotgun. He stopped and again stood as still as a hunter. Now turning his head and stooping, he looked back at the fence.
> But he had not forgotten anything.[19]

What comes swimming up from deep inside him is a memory of such singular force that when it emerges Will not only vividly recalls what he had tried so hard to forget, but realizes it has ruled his life for so long that it is as if it was the only thing that had ever happened to him. What Will remembers is a hunting trip he had taken with his father when he was twelve years old. It was the hunting trip on which his father, after telling Will, "You are like me. We are two of a kind," had tried to kill himself.[20]

With that act the demon of the father passed into the son. The hunting trip had been planned to let Will in on a secret: Death is more real than life. Death is the truth of things and someday Will, like his father, will have to give death its due, paying it homage by taking his own life. Thinking back on that day, Barrett asks, in silent conversation with his father, "For that was your secret, wasn't it? That it was death you loved most of all and loved so surely that you wanted to share the secret with me because you loved me too."[21]

His father failed to kill himself that weekend; later he was successful. His message to Will was that he had inherited the dark but true secret of his father. Unlike the multitudes who either did not know or would not acknowledge the sovereignty of death, Will knew the secret, Will knew the deep-down truth of things, and someday Will, like his father, would have to act on what he knew, honoring death by putting a bullet in his brain. The fatal destiny of the father would be the fatal destiny of the son, that was the sacred bond between them, that was Will's inheritance. As his father saw it, embracing this truth was not some morbid sickness-unto-death, but the clear, steady vision of one who sees things as they really are and has the courage not to look away. That Will too would one day be called to honor death by sacrificing himself in suicide was the price he must pay for the secret that had been bequeathed to him. The son's fate was to be as wrapped up in death as the father.

Embracing a Mythology of Death

Death is what Will's father loved most. It seems strange, unnatural, even perverse to speak of loving death, but if death is more real than life and life little more than death disguised, it makes sad sense. Everything in the moral life hinges on these questions: What is the truth of things? What is the force standing behind life? Is it life or is it death? How we live, perceive, choose, feel, and act pivots on how we answer these questions. If we see the world through the prism of death, then death, not life, will be the power informing everything we do, the shadow throwing itself across our consciousness. If we come to believe that death is more real than life and, therefore, will ultimately prevail over life, our attitudes and actions will reflect this. All of us are governed by some basic interpretation of life that is both reflected in and furthered by our actions.[22] If we embrace a mythology of life, a deep conviction that life, despite its inevitable hardships and disappointments, is graced, trustworthy, promising, and good, everything about us will witness this. Our actions will communicate what we deeply believe, each of them testimony to our conviction that life may not be easy, but it is, nonetheless, blessed and full of hope.

But what happens if ours is not a mythology of life but of death? How are we formed — what happens to us — if we are secretly convinced that life is not graced, people cannot be trusted, and the world is filled with more enemies than friends? If we live by a mythology of death, this too will be communicated in everything about us — our speech, our values, our attitudes and actions, our relationships, and even our everyday interactions with others. Sometimes, sadly enough, people have ample reasons to believe death is more real than life. It is how life has come home to them; it is what has been chiseled into the center of their hearts. It is hard for them to have confidence in the goodness of life because so little in their experience confirms it. The world for them has not been awash in beauty and grace, but in exploitation and pain. Contrary to the resurrection, life has not lifted them up, it has beaten them down.

Sometimes their misfortune is a matter of bad luck — things go wrong and there is little they can do about it — but other times it is the harvest of all the wrong that has been done to them by the thoughtlessness and cruelty and indifference of others. Life has come home to them not as a gift to be embraced but as a curse to be endured. Theirs has been a history not of love and promise and goodness and kindness, but of hurt, betrayal, abuse, disappointment, and despair. They are mired in a pit of hopelessness not because they have chosen it, but because the injustice of others keeps pushing them down.

Will Barrett's father's secret love of death may be a tragic perversion of everything life is meant to be, but it is not a rare one. There are many secret lovers of death, many who belong to the hopeless confraternity of those who believe death is more real than life, not because they wish things to be this way but because so much in their lives has convinced them it cannot be otherwise. The force of life has been an endless denial of themselves and their dreams, a crushing demolition of all their hopes. Sometimes it is the work of unexpected misfortune: sickness, loss of employment, the sudden death of a family member or friend. Other times it is the work of another's evil: constant belittlement, physical or emotional abuse, infidelity and betrayal, vengeance and vindictiveness, lying and deceit, or simply the selfishness with which we can beat one another down. For many people life is not ultimately good or affirming, but painfully negating, and that is why they see the force of death standing behind everything, sovereign over all.

But there are also some who become lovers of death not on account of the adversity they suffer, but because they refuse to make choices that will bring them life. They close themselves to grace, they develop all kinds of elaborate strategies to avoid anything that would make them grow or offer them hope. Instead of life-affirming virtues such as love and joy and truthfulness and hope, they nurture the death-dealing vices of cynicism and envy and resentment and bitterness. They mock anything positive and ridicule anything hopeful. And although they boast that they are the realists, the truth is they are ruled by fear and falsehood. They are desperately afraid of challenge and opportunity and change, and absolutely terrified of grace and new life. They love the tombs they have made for themselves and, shut up in that darkness, have no idea life is passing them by.

Part of the merit of *The Second Coming* is that it helps us see why lives entombed in a mythology of death are a serious moral problem we cannot ignore. It makes us realize how many in our world are controlled by something which robs them of the life God wants us all to have. Morality grows from our most basic convictions about life and the world. If people believe death is more real than life, and life, therefore, can be nothing more than death-in-life, they are held bound by a hopeless gospel that will destroy them. They unfailingly make choices for death because they are ineluctably turned toward it, sucked up by its evil energy. Death holds sway over them — they truly are under its dominion — which is why all their choices further despair. Locked tight in a narrative of death, they see all of reality tilted to negation. It is no wonder that for them Easter seems at best a fairy tale, at worst a cruel lie, and not the deep-down truth of things.

Will Barrett's father lived the mythology of death to its most logical, but tragic, conclusion: in an attic in Mississippi he put a double-barreled shotgun in his mouth and blew his brains away. There was a certain logic to his deed if death, not life, is the truth of things. If what abides is not life and goodness and love, but nothingness and negation, then to kill oneself is to understand. For Barrett's father life was not real, only death and death-in-life; for him, at the heart of life lurked nothingness. This was why his father believed there was no way to escape "the great suck of self" and no reason to try. Life is governed not by a God of love and grace and blessings, but by the Great Depriver, the one whose heart is darkness and whose delight is to diminish and destroy.

To love or to despair? This is not only a key question of the novel but also a key question of life each of us finally must answer. To love or to despair? For Walker Percy they are our alternatives, and consciously or not each of us endorses one or the other each day through our attitudes and actions. As Percy sees it, if we are convinced that death rules life and that in the end death alone abides, then the ultimate ecstasy is not to go out of oneself in love, but to turn utterly in on oneself in cynicism and despair. To love or to despair? This is the question everyone confronts and how we answer it determines the plot of our lives. Barrett's father answered it in an act of absolute hopelessness. His suicide was his final homage to the mythology of death, an act that left the demons laughing. In a particularly disturbing passage, Will Barrett describes his father's suicide as a profoundly perverted love act. It is not the act of love by which we are drawn out of ourself and into union with another, but the act by which we can turn so completely in on ourself in despair that we finally disappear into nothingness.

I remember now. I cleaned the gun when I got it back from the sheriff in Mississippi. Both barrels. Wouldn't one have been enough? Yes, given an ordinary need for death. But not if it's a love of death. In the case of love, more is better than less, two twice as good as one, and most is best of all. And if the aim is the ecstasy of love, two is closer to infinity than one, especially when the two are twelve-gauge Super-X number-eight shot. And what samurai self-love of death . . . can match the double Winchester come of taking oneself into oneself, the cold-steel extension of oneself into mouth . . . the penetration and union of perfect cold gunmetal into warm quailing mortal flesh, the coming to end all coming, brain cells which together faltered and fell short, now flowered and flew apart, flung like stars around the whole dark world.[23]

In Search of Something More than Death

Barrett's father's suicide was the culmination of his principal conviction: there is not life; there is only death and death-in-life. But the son wonders if his father was mistaken. Did he settle for less than he ought? Did his suicide represent not the final truth of things, but a horrible error in perception? Will cannot help but wonder if his father failed to search far enough. If there is in the end only death and death-in-life, his father's suicide was fitting. But his father might have been deceived and maybe even cowardly. Will cannot passively accept his father's destiny as his own. He must find out for himself if there is something more, something hopeful, something beautifully promising to life. Like his father he, too, has known death-in-life, but unlike his father he is not yet willing to accept this sad reality as final. What if there is life? Not death-in-life but life?

These are the questions prompting Will's disquietude and guiding his search. His father was disenchanted, but instead of rebelling he only despaired. Will's disenchantment, however, leads him not to cynicism and hopelessness, but to question and explore. If he must settle for death so be it, but he first needs to know if there can be something more. "Ah, but what if there is another way?" he asks his father. "Maybe that was your mistake, that you didn't even look. That's the difference between us. I'm going to find out once and for all. You never even looked."[24]

But not every search takes us to hopeful places. Barrett first tries to break free of the death-dealing destiny of his father by marrying, practicing law in an office on Wall Street, keeping a sailboat, playing squash, and walking his poodle in the park. He rejects his father's death-in-life by embracing what our society says is the perfectly happy life. His objective was to flee as far as possible from his father's allegiance to death by emulating what nearly everyone says constitutes a successful and fulfilling life. The cure for his father's death-obsessed life would be to "live an ordinary mild mercantile money-making life, do mild sailing, mild poodle-walking, mild music-loving among mild good natured folks."[25] The aim of this mild and decent life was to free Will from the ghost of his father and the secret he had bequeathed him.

But it didn't work. Will tried to break free from his past and his father's deadly hold on him by shaping a life as far different from his father's as possible. He left the south, married Marion of Utica, New York, made more money than most, went to the theater, and learned to love Mozart and Brahms. He had hoped "there would be something different out there, different from death, maybe even a kind of life,"[26] but what he found was not the kind of life for which he was searching, and not the kind of life that could free him from death. He did all the right things but still felt more dead than alive. He tried to escape his father's intoxication with death by taking up a completely different life, but what he was looking for was not to be found in his Wall Street office or at the theater or while walking his poodle in the park. "In two seconds he saw that his little Yankee life had not worked after all," Percy writes, "the nearly twenty years of making a life with a decent upstate woman and with decent Northern folk and working in an honorable Wall Street firm and making a success of it too."[27] Now Marion is dead, Wall Street is behind him, and he finds himself in North Carolina thinking of the Jews, looking for a sign, falling down on golf courses and wondering: "What in God's name was I doing there, and am I doing here?"[28]

His first search for life was a dead-end, leaving Will to wonder if his father's diagnosis was right after all. Is there no escaping the dominion of death? Does it finally trump our every attempt at life? "That day in the swamp you were trying to tell me that this was what it was going to come to, not only for you but in the end for me, weren't you?," Barrett muses. "It's not your fault that after all this time here I am back where we started and you ended, that there is after all no escaping it for us."[29] Will is still held bound by the tentacles of death, forced to ask if his failed attempt to escape the dominion of death means his father was right and there is no true path to life, just the endless saga of death-in-life. He did not find life where everyone says it can and will be found; pleasure and success maybe, but not freedom and life.

Will made one discovery (his New York life was not the answer), but he needs to make another one. If his first search took him to Wall Street, his second search has him looking for golf balls in the North Carolina rough. He will make a discovery there too, and it will be the start of his resurrection. Barrett will move from a mythology of death to a mythology of life not by being a successful Wall Street lawyer, but by falling into a love eager to receive him. To despair or to love? So far everything makes Will think his life must be a tragic replay of his father's. But that will change when he wanders into the rough and finds there not his golf ball, but Allison Vaught in her greenhouse.

Why Love Is the Only Power We Have Over Darkness and Death

Will tumbles into Allison's greenhouse when his scheme to make the Great Discovery goes awry. Having concluded that his father's suicide was wasted, an act that proved nothing and did nobody good, Will concocts "one of the strangest schemes ever hit upon by the mind of man."[30] His plan is to descend into the depths of Lost Cove cave, an old Civil War hiding place bordering the golf course, and stay there until God gives a sign proving his existence. If God reveals himself before Will dies, God's existence will be certain. On the other hand, if Will dies in Lost Cove cave with nary a whisper from God, at least his death will have achieved some good: through him the world can be certain that God does not exist. In a letter to Dr. Sutter Vaught, Allison's uncle, Will explains his strategy:

> My project is the first scientific experiment in history to settle once and for all the question of God's existence. As things presently stand, there may be signs of his existence but they point both ways and are therefore ambiguous and so prove nothing....
>
> No more *deus absconditus!*
>
> Come out, come out, wherever you are, the game's over.
>
> No, I do not mean to joke. What I am doing is asking God with the utmost respect to break his silence....
>
> My experiment is simply this: I shall go to a desert place and wait for God to give a sign. If no sign is forthcoming I shall die. But people will know why I died: because there is no sign. The cause of my death will be either his nonexistence or his refusal to manifest himself, which comes to the same thing as far as we are concerned. Only you know the nature of the experiment. I give you permission to publish the results in a scientific journal of your choice.[31]

Barrett's lifelines could not have been bent further. What began as an aberrant golf shot which took him into the rough, ends as a crackpot scheme to draw God out of hiding. How could it be that a man who had been blessed with "a fairly normal life, a fairly happy marriage, a successful career, and a triumphant early retirement to enjoy the good things of life" was now "more funked out and nuttier than ever"?[32] Something is seriously amiss. Here is a man who keeps falling down in a world he is convinced is falling apart; and yet one cannot help but ask if the crisis which draws Will Barrett to Lost Cove cave reflects a deeper crisis in our world. Barrett retreats to the cave not only because once and for all he wants to establish the existence of God, but also because he cannot endure a world gone mad without God.

His quest to make the Great Discovery witnesses a disenchantment gone wild. Like Isaiah and Amos and other prophets before him, Will's dismay with the customary and conventional has opened his eyes to a new and different way of looking at the world. He does not see as most people do but with the searing and disturbing vision of a prophet, and that may be his hope. Beneath the veneer of a good life amidst good people who "worked hard, made money, raised families, [had] been good citizens, and now were able to enjoy summer places or retire into condos and villas and savor the fruits of their labors,"[33] Will sees the darkness and despair of the modern world in people who "while professing a love of peace and freedom and life, secretly . . . loved war and thralldom and death."[34]

And so Will's descent into the depths of Lost Cove is not only a dramatic — and prophetic? — sign of his radical rejection of a life he finds killing, but also testifies how far his exile from ordinary life has taken him. In what Percy calls "the strangest adventure of his life," Will sets out to find God by crawling into the darkness of a cave. Midway through the novel, Will Barrett entombs himself in darkness in order to escape a world he's convinced has gone mad. Percy leaves us wondering who is crazier, a more than middle-aged man who crawls into caves looking for God, or a people who use their gifts and creativity to devise increasingly efficient ways to destroy.

> So it was that Will Barrett went mad. His peculiar delusion and the strange pass it brought him to would be comical if it were not so perilous. This unfortunate man, long subject to "spells," "petty-mall" trances, and such minor disorders, had now gone properly crazy. This is how crazy he was. He had become convinced that the Last Days were at hand, that the world had fallen into the hands of the only species which knew how to destroy itself along with all other living creatures on earth, that whenever in history this species had invented a weapon, it had forthwith used it; that it was characteristic of this species that, through a perversity or an upsidedownness peculiar to it, while professing a love of peace and freedom and life, secretly it loved war and thralldom and death and loved them to a degree that it, the species, in these last days behaved like creatures possessed by demons; that the end would come by fire, a fire such as had not been seen in all of history until this century of demons, a fire which would consume the earth. . . .

Madness! Madness! Madness! Yet such was the nature of Will Barrett's peculiar delusion when he left his comfortable home atop a pleasant Carolina mountain and set forth on the strangest adventure of his life, descended into Lost Cove cave looking for proof of the existence of God and a sign of the apocalypse like some crackpot preacher in California.[35]

Out of the Cave and into the Greenhouse

Alas, Barrett's Grand Discovery is cut short by a toothache, one of those unforeseen distractions which make it extremely difficult to focus on cosmic questions. With the pain from the toothache throbbing in his brain, Barrett forgets about proving the existence of God; all he wants is to find his way out of the cave as quickly as possible. And he succeeds, but only by getting lost. Stumbling in absolute darkness, overcome with pain and nausea, he wanders off the path on which he entered Lost Cove cave, exiting not where his journey began, but by falling headfirst into Allison's greenhouse.

The greenhouse was Allison's home. Hidden in the woods bordering the golf course, the greenhouse was part of a plot of land she had inherited from her aunt. Allison moved into the greenhouse after her escape from the hospital and had already encountered Will Barrett a few times when he wandered into the rough in search of a stray golf ball. The greenhouse was built around an opening in Lost Cove cave from which flowed a steady rush of cool air which kept the temperature stable each season of the year. It was from this vine-shrouded opening that Will came tumbling out of the blinding darkness of the cave into the blinding light of the greenhouse. That a greenhouse is a place of light and life — a place where things are nurtured and grow — alerts us that it will be the place of Will's rebirth and resurrection.

When Will falls into Allison's greenhouse he is nearly dead. Severely weakened from his days in Lost Cove cave and unconscious from his fall, to Allison he "smelled of a freshly dug ditch. A grave."[36] He was "smeared with clay and bent double."[37] These images suggest one who has died and is just now coming back to life. Barrett's fall into the greenhouse marks the start of his "second coming." If his descent into the cave signaled his death to a life he found killing, his tumble into Allison's greenhouse is his fall back into grace because it is with her that he will be gradually brought back to life.

The parallel to Christ's death, burial, and resurrection could not be more striking. Easter images are everywhere. Barrett makes his own paschal passage when he is entombed in Lost Cove cave and moves from death to resurrection by falling into Allison's life. He who tumbles from the darkness of the cave into the light of her world is being born again, not to repeat the life he sought to escape, but to discover something blessed, something gracious. Percy's description of Barrett as one who was "smeared with clay and bent double" suggests newly born life emerging from the womb.

With his unplanned exit from the cave, God's gracious providence is once more at work. Having lost his way, Will Barrett is found by a God who works through a woman everyone thinks is crazy. Throughout the novel Barrett has been looking for a sign, seeking some assurance of the love and existence of God, and in ways he cannot yet realize he has found that sign not in Lost Cove cave but in Allison. It is with and through Allison that death's hold over him shall be broken.

When he first enters her world, Barrett is like a newborn baby, a helpless, defenseless child. Unable to care for himself, Allison must do everything: bathe him, clothe him, feed him. She has a gift for restoration, and having restored the greenhouse and made it her home, she will also restore Will. Percy comments that Allison has a knack for hoisting, for putting things upright and in their proper place, and so it shall be with Will. She will help him find his "proper place" in life — where he fits and truly belongs — and she will do so through love.

But Allison will also find healing and life through Will. She will find it first by caring for Will. To her surprise, Allison likes caring for Barrett. It makes her happy, it gives her life purpose and direction. By nurturing Will, Allison herself grows stronger and healthier so that as she gives him life she receives life. But it works the other way too. Allison also finds healing and life by being loved and cared for by Will; it is the *giving and receiving* that brings her back to life.

Love will be the power of their mutual restoration, the giving and receiving of care, affection, attentiveness, and delight that achieves their gradual re-creation, their second coming to life. Allison remembers when she was in grade school she heard people talking about "doing it," and wonders if "doing it" is "the secret of life? Is this," she asks, "a secret everyone knows but no one talks about?"[38] "Was there something she did not know and needed to be told? Perhaps it was a matter of 'falling in love.'"[39] It occurs to her that she "knew a great deal about pulleys and hoists but nothing about love," and so she goes to the library "to look up love as she had looked up the mechanical advantages of pulleys."[40]

Percy answers that, yes, "doing it" is the secret of life, that falling in love and living in love is the secret everyone needs to learn if they are to have life, real life, not death-in-life. But Allison will learn about love not by looking it up in the library, but by caring for Will and by being cared for by him. Like Barrett, she will be brought to wholeness through all the ordinariness of everyday faithful love.

This is where the tone of the novel shifts. If before Will and Allison seemed caught in a trance of depression and death, when he crashes into her greenhouse and into her arms the mood immediately changes. If before everything had the feel of oppression and gloom born from despair, now there is an Easter morning feeling of hope, fresh life, beauty, and joy. Like all first signs of life, it may be fragile and small, a tiny bud just breaking through the thawing earth, but it is nonetheless real. Thus, the reader is not surprised that Allison, when reading from *The Trail of the Lonesome Pine*, an old novel she found in the greenhouse, is drawn to a passage that speaks of "the first sign of spring."[41]

Coming Back to Life through Love

There are many signs of new life in Allison. If before she felt a misfit in a world she neither understood nor wanted, through caring for Will — running errands for him, shopping for him, nursing him back to health — Allison receives not only a stronger sense of who she is but, perhaps more importantly, a sense of belonging. A world that once seemed strange and forbidding is seen in a new way; to Allison it looks warm and welcoming now, even lovely. Instead of feeling awkward and unsure about making her way in this world (wondering if everyone else was in on a secret she did not know), Allison begins to feel at home. It is a feeling that takes her by surprise, but one she joyfully embraces: "She sat on her bench but in a new way. The buildings and the stores were the same but more accessible.... She was a piece of the world after all, a member of a class and recognizable as such. I belong here!"[42]

"I belong here!" Those words are Allison's liberation cry and when she utters them the reader wants to cheer. This woman who had "made straight A's and flunked ordinary living" is coming back to life through love. Being with Will changes her sense of herself and her sense of life; with him to love and to be loved by, life looks different, more hopeful and inviting. "How good life must be once you got the hang of it,"[43] she reflects, and for Allison "getting the hang" of life was a matter of finding someone to love and to be loved by. The world looks lovely now not because it was ungraced and forsaken before, but because only now is Allison able to see its beauty and its promise. She sees the world through her love for Will, that is why everything ordinary shines in new luster. Life looks different to her not because the world has changed, but because Allison's vision of it has. Everything looks different when viewed through a vision of gratitude and love, of reverence and appreciation. The transformation Allison senses in the world is more accurately a deep transformation in herself wrought through the sheer graciousness of love. Life looks inviting, absolutely appealing and full of grace, not because it has been created anew, but because Allison has.

Allison is happy for the first time in her life. She discovers that joy comes through love, not the false and empty loves that deplete us, but the good and promising loves that fill us with life. Allison's good and promising love is with Will and she knows it: "[T]he thought of marrying him made her grin and skip like a schoolgirl. . . . She could look at a doodlebug with him and be happy."[44] Her life will be defined and fulfilled by being together with him, and he will be healed and restored through her. Each is a reason for the other's resurrection, each the other's path out of the tomb. Will and Allison will know Easter, but it will come to them in and through the love they offer one another.

Allison and Will find life through the love that flows between them. Each becomes a home for the other. This is expressed beautifully in a scene in which Allison's love really does bring Will back to life. Late one afternoon she finds him near the spring by the greenhouse, fallen, trembling from the cold and unable to get up. At first she wonders if he is dead. Lying on him to gain leverage for pulling him up, Allison says, "Don't worry, I'll get you back."[45] Staggering, she carries him to the greenhouse and rolls him onto the bunk. She removes his wet clothes, lies on top of him, and uses the warmth of her body to draw him back to life. It is a beautiful image, her life passing into him and keeping him from death. Allison resurrects Will through the warmth and power of love; it is the gift that saves him.

> There was nothing for her to do now but, spent, gasping, trembling, use her last strength and climb over him, cover them with the sleeping bag and hold him until she got stronger and he stopped shivering. Somehow she, they, got them undressed, his wet clothes her dry clothes off, her warm body curled around his lard-cold muscle straps and bones, spoon-nesting him, her knees coming up behind him until he was shivering less and, signaling a turn, he nested her, encircled her as if he were her cold dead planet and she his sun's warmth.[46]

Allison and Will make love, each giving life back to the other. "She was moving against him, enclosing him, wrapping her arms and legs around him," Percy writes, "as if her body had at last found the center of itself outside itself."[47] Percy suggests we are made to yield to one another, created to place our lives in communion with others, because our center of life is not in ourselves, but in others, and ultimately, of course, in God. This is why if we turn in on ourself we die, why if we never learn to risk, to give, and to be open enough to receive another in friendship and love we fashion our own hell of loneliness and hopelessness. If the Eucharist tells us anything, it tells us we are made for friendship and communion, not isolation and estrangement, and that we find happiness and life only to the degree that we move out of ourself and into communion with God and others through love.

The message of *The Second Coming* is to show us that we overcome the powers of death through love. Death-in-life is conquered by the love that draws us out of ourselves and into relationships with others. It is love seeking communion that gives us life. It is in handing ourself over to another in love — loving them generously, graciously, and joyfully, and being loved by them in return — that we finally escape the everlasting suck of self that wearies and destroys, and ultimately leaves us with nothing but our own desperate despair. Through Will and Allison, Percy suggests that we find ourself in others, that we come to life not through selfishness and guardedness, not through suspicion and mistrust, and not through the ambiguous security of power and wealth, but through the dazzling creativity of generous mutual love. We are made to give and to yield, to offer and to receive, the gift of each one's self seeking communion with another. This is how life triumphs over death; this is the only way to real liberation.

Why Love Is All We Have against Death

Loving another and being loved by them is life for us. There is no escaping this because it is only by learning to love and living in love that we can have life at all. In *The Second Coming* Percy demonstrates that human beings have more than a bent for love, we have an absolute need for it. Human beings are created *from love* and *for love*, it is the heart and soul of our being, it is the innermost secret of who we are. To live we have to love, there is no other way to be, which is why failure to love diminishes and never loving kills. We shrivel when we hate, we grow cold when we hold grudges, we become brittle and bitter when we refuse to forgive. Only through loving and being loved can we grow as graced human beings, as living, breathing images of God. If we are made to love one another, we die when we don't, which is why hardened hearts are not only regrettable, they are fatal. To live is to love and to love is to live — this is why love is all we have against death and the only power strong enough to shatter darkness. Love and life can never be separated because not to love and not to be loved is to die. What Allison and Will discover is that there is no way other than love for the shackles of death to be broken.

The plot of *The Second Coming* is to show us how to be freed from the disabling power of death in all of its wily manifestations. Death is dethroned by love — this is the message Walker Percy shouts to us in the death-to-life story of Will Barrett and Allison Vaught. If our most basic moral task is to choose life over death, we do so insofar as we love others and are loved by them. Failures to love and refusals to be loved lead to lives ensconced in sometimes cozy but always suffocating tombs. True, there are things which steal our life away, but we are not powerless before them. True, there are things that deepen brokenness

and rupture what is meant to be one, but broken hearts, broken relationships, and broken worlds can be made whole. It all depends on
whether we *live into Easter* or *into death*.

Love has power over death. This is the message of *The Second Coming*, the heart of the Easter gospel, and the innermost truth of life. It
is the discovery both Will and Allison make, and it is what finally sets
them free. This is captured poignantly in a memorable scene in the
novel when Will decides to perform a grand exorcism on himself.

As with any exorcism, Will can be freed from the "demons" which
possess him only by first naming them. He must "name the enemy"
because only then can he break free of the powers of darkness and
death ruling over him. The same is true for us. In order to move from
death to life and from darkness into light, we must be able to name
the things which steal our life away and keep us from being free. We
gain power over things which diminish and debilitate not when we
suppress or deny them, but when we have the courage to see them for
what they are and deal truthfully with them. What are the "enemies"
possessing us? What are the destructive powers which sometimes rule
our souls? What are the things that keep us from being free? That
bring us death-in-life, not life? As Barrett observes at the start of his
own exorcism, "Ha, there is a secret after all. . . . But to know the secret
answer, you must first know the secret question. The question is, who
is the enemy? Not to know the name of the enemy is already to have
been killed by him."[48] And for Barrett the name of the enemy is death,
"not the death people die but the death people live."[49]

Having found life with Allison, Barrett refuses ever again to be
mastered by death. The climactic scene of *The Second Coming* is Will's
self-performed exorcism because through it he is released from the
tyranny of death to enjoy, for the first time, the beauty and goodness of
life. He has discovered that to be death-possessed, to live in the power
of the Great Depriver, is to surrender our lives to a tragic falsehood.
According to Percy, the great cosmic lie is that death is more real
than life, that death, not life, is the truth of things, and that death,
in all its multiple disguises, ultimately prevails. The cunning strategy
of evil, at work from the beginning of time, is to convince us of the
inescapable sovereignty of death; indeed, it is to encourage in us a taste
for what is deadly: "Old father of lies, that's what you are, the devil

himself," Barrett proclaims in prophetic splendor, "for only the devil could have thought up all the deceits and guises under which death masquerades."[50]

The power of this novel is to demonstrate how easy it is for us to be seduced by all the stratagems of death and to be bewitched by the lie that death, not life, is the truth of things. But even more so, its power is to show us how tragically sad it is when this happens to anyone. The story of Will and Allison's release from death-in-life is an Easter story because it powerfully unmasks all the pretensions of death. It is an Easter story because its heartfelt claim is that death is not where the power is; the power is with life, a life that is born from God's gracious and merciful love, and a life that is stronger than all the crafty manifestations of death. Realizing this, Will chooses life, and in that choice for life renounces death in all of its forms, refusing ever again to be mastered by them. "It is a matter of knowing and choosing," he says. "To know the many names of death is also to know there is life. I choose life.... Death in none of its guises shall prevail over me because I know all the names of death."[51]

Percy wants us to choose life too and choosing life is *essentially* what the moral life is all about. But in order to choose life we first have to know "the many names of death." What brings death to us? What steals our life away? What leaves us resigned to sadness? And once we have named the demons which possess us, whether they be hurtful memories, other people, or our own sinfulness, we must, with the help of God's grace and those who love us, strive to be free. If in our lives death seems to be winning, we should never accept it; such resignation spells the end of hope and the certainty of defeat. If something is bleeding our lives away, whether it be injustice, another person's cruelty, a crippling sadness that has settled on our hearts, or a poisonous bitterness and anger, we should never grow complacent; rather, like Will and Allison, we should rebel, seeking to overcome the dominion of death by exposing it for the lie it is. Percy's point is the gospel's point: We should overthrow all the things which crush and diminish. We should dethrone all the powers that violate and destroy.

God calls us not to the tomb but to fullness of life, which is why we should never tolerate all the life-robbing forces which work to dominate and destroy. Death-in-life is tempting and it is not rare, but there is another way. Christians call it Easter, and Easter is the feast that ought to be a way of life. We are called to live in the power of Easter each day, not simply commemorate it once a year. Christ calls us to a paschal existence, and we cheat ourselves — and grieve God — if we settle for anything less.

Finding the God behind Love

Will went into Lost Cove cave on a journey to find God but found a toothache instead. The toothache led him to Allison, Allison led him to love, and love led him to life. But has Will Barrett found God? Percy suggests God has been there all along, working through the most ordinary and incidental things of life, like golf swings and toothaches, to reach Will. Throughout the novel Barrett has been on the lookout for signs, searching for anything that points him to God. He has wanted to prove the existence of God, but what he realizes now is that signs of God's presence abound if only we have eyes to see. God lives in all things, even in the strangest of places and in the most unlikely characters; we do not have to prove the existence of God, only discover it. We live in a sacramental universe, a universe in which God beckons to us every day in the beauty of nature, in the faces of strangers, in the cries of the poor, and in the straightforward goodness of people like Allison, if we only learn to see.

Near the end of the novel Will Barrett discovers God existing in one final and surprising way. He is drawn to Fr. Weatherbee, a doddering priest who wants nothing more than to spend his last days in the attic of a nursing home playing with model trains. Will goes to him because he senses the old priest has "the authority to tell me something I don't know."[52] Will is convinced Fr. Weatherbee knows something important, that he may be the bearer of a life-saving secret, so he tells the old priest he will not leave him alone until he shares this secret with him. Fr. Weatherbee responds by telling Will a story of his missionary work in Mindanao. He remembers that even though the people in his tiny village were "as poor as any people on earth," they joyfully embraced the gospel he brought to them *as if their lives depended on its truth*. As the old priest remembers, "They believed me! They believed the Gospel whole and entire, and the teachings of the church. They said that if I told them, then it must be true or I would not have gone to so much trouble."[53]

The good news of *The Second Coming* — and the good news of life — is that there is a gospel and what it says is true: Behind all the darkness and death, behind all the sadness and tragedy of life, stands a power of love that will not be overcome. Behind all the struggles and losses of life, behind everything tempting us to despair, stands a grace and a peace that is not some utopian dream, but *the truth we are meant to live.* All hope starts with Easter, and Easter is not some future fancy, but an already established fact.

Allison's and Will's love can be trusted because it is rooted in and dependent on a God whose love is stronger than death. It is the love of a God crucified but risen, the love of a God who breaks the bonds of death and shatters the darkness forever. Allison is a gift, but Will's final discovery is to learn through Fr. Weatherbee that behind every gift stands a gift giver, a God who continually surprises us with gifts of love. Will has had many of them in *The Second Coming*, most of all in Allison. Allison is a sacrament of a gift-giving God, but God gives life-saving gifts all the time if only we wake up (or, like Will Barrett, fall down) and see. At the end of the novel, Will looks into Fr. Weatherbee's eyes, thinks of Allison, and asks,

> What is it I want from her and him, he wondered, not only want but must have? Is she a gift and therefore a sign of a giver? Could it be that the Lord is here, masquerading behind this simple silly holy face? Am I crazy to want both her and Him? No, not want, must have. And will have.[54]

Are the demons laughing? Only if we let them. We can choose death, we can even revel in it, but if we do we should at least be honest enough to confess that we are living at odds with the pulse of the universe. Life will win out, grace will prevail, and goodness will overcome evil all because "the one who was crucified has been raised up" (Mk 16:6). Easter is a feast that is meant to be a way of life. If *The Second Coming* tells us anything, it tells us our most basic moral choice, indeed our most crucial one, is to live the feast we have been given.

In this chapter we have explored why the heart of morality is the challenge to choose life over death each day. Life is stronger than death, but we discover this only when we risk love with others just as God, in sending his son, risked love with us. In addition to Walker Percy, the following authors have explored this theme as well. Some, like Percy, show how love and goodness can shatter darkness in our lives. Others, however, tell stories of how darkness and death triumph in people who never respond to the invitation to love.

Bausch, Richard, *Real Presence*
Dostoyevsky, Fyodor, *Crime and Punishment*
————, *The Brothers Karamazov*
Fitzgerald, F. Scott, *The Great Gatsby*
Haruf, Kent, *Plainsong*
Hassler, Jon, *North of Hope*
————, *Simon's Night*
Ishiguro, Kazuo, *The Remains of the Day*
Kingsolver, Barbara, *Pigs In Heaven*
Morrison, Toni, *Beloved*
O'Connor, Flannery, *The Violent Bear It Away*
————, *Wise Blood*
Powers, J. F., *Morte D'Urban*
Salinger, J. D., *The Catcher in the Rye*
Tolstoy, Leo, *The Death of Ivan Ilych*
Walker, Alice, *The Color Purple*
Williams, Tennessee, *A Streetcar Named Desire*
————, *The Night of the Iguana*
Wolfe, Tom, *A Man in Full*
————, *The Bonfire of the Vanities*

Notes

1. Walker Percy, *The Second Coming* (New York: Pocket Books, 1980). Subsequent page references to the novel refer to this a edition only. Different editions, of course, will have different page references.

2. Percy, 3. **3.** Percy, 4. **4.** Percy, 3. **5.** Percy, 3. **6.** Percy, 4. **7.** Percy, 18. **8.** Percy, 53. **9.** Percy, 78. **10.** Percy, 40. **11.** Percy, 28. **12.** Percy, 31. **13.** Percy, 37. **14.** Percy, 108. **15.** Percy, 108. **16.** Percy, 108. **17.** Percy, 35–36. **18.** Percy, 63–64. **19.** Percy, 59. **20.** Percy, 66. **21.** Percy, 146.

22. For a fuller treatment of this theme, see H. Richard Niebuhr, *The Responsible Self* (New York: Harper & Row, 1963).

23. Percy, 172. **24.** Percy, 153. **25.** Percy, 84. **26.** Percy, 83. **27.** Percy, 84. **28.** Percy, 85. **29.** Percy, 85. **30.** Percy, 210. **31.** Percy, 222–24. **32.** Percy, 208–9. **33.** Percy, 209. **34.** Percy, 229. **35.** Percy, 228–29. **36.** Percy, 268. **37.** Percy, 268. **38.** Percy, 274. **39.** Percy, 275. **40.** Percy, 275. **41.** Percy, 273. **42.** Percy, 283–85. **43.** Percy, 289. **44.** Percy, 290. **45.** Percy, 293. **46.** Percy, 293. **47.** Percy, 295. **48.** Percy, 311. **49.** Percy, 311. **50.** Percy, 311–12. **51.** Percy, 314. **52.** Percy, 409. **53.** Percy, 410. **54.** Percy, 411.

CHAPTER TWO

LIVING OUTSIDE OF EDEN

Why There's Hope for the Wayward

W E ARE A LONG WAY FROM EDEN. Anyone who reflects honestly on our human condition, especially our penchant for mischief and deceit, knows our innocence was lost the moment the first human couple swallowed a serpent's lie. Created for goodness and with the path to happiness laid right out before us, we've instead become experts at making a mess of things, most often our own lives. Who of us understands our own hearts? Why are we so good at self-sabotage? Why do we consistently fall short of the love and goodness for which we are made? Why do we sometimes stumble more than we soar? Why do we know more scoundrels than saints?

Many authors have attempted to answer these questions, but perhaps none more expertly than Graham Greene. He's a master at depicting the depths of human brokenness and the ease with which we stray. His novels are filled with characters who want to do good, but somehow lose their center. It's as if the farther we are from paradise, the easier it is to fall. This is especially true in *The Heart of the Matter*, Greene's novel about human pettiness, meanness, and corruption, which suggests if there ever was a paradise where perfection was possible and harm unknown, it's part of a galaxy we can never retrieve.

Consider how the novel begins. Wilson, a government accountant, has just arrived in a remote British colony in West Africa. It is Sunday morning, the day of the Lord, but there is nothing at all in this opening scene to suggest the presence of God. Wilson sits on the balcony of the Bedford Hotel, sipping gin and watching life unfold beneath him. Greene describes him as already feeling "almost intolerably lonely."[1]

As the cathedral bell clangs for matins, a vulture flies off the corrugated iron roof above him. There are people going to church, but what catches Wilson's eye are some young boys trying to lure a few sailors to prostitutes. Harris, who has been in the colony "eighteen bloody months,"[2] appears and Wilson asks if he will soon be going home. Harris responds, "The ships all go the wrong way. But when I do get home you'll never see me here again. . . . I hate the place. I hate the people."[3]

In this opening scene, Greene paints a picture. This harsh and dreary colony where it is always unbearably hot, where rats roam freely and vultures are everywhere, where everyone seems lonely, lost, and exhausted, is a metaphor for a fallen humanity in a fallen world. We are clearly a long way from Eden. This is no lush garden brimming with life, but a desolate place where one sips gin in the morning to help get through the rest of the day. And that Wilson has just arrived "from home" suggests the colony is a place of exile, haven for the shipwrecked. Dropped onto shores they can never call home, they are aliens stuck in a place that seems oppressively unblessed. The relentless tropical heat, the constant swarming of mosquitoes, the sudden fall to exotic diseases are all reminders that paradise is oceans away.

What is the fate of the shipwrecked? What will happen to the misbegotten? The characters of *The Heart of the Matter* are a fallen people stumbling about in a fallen world. Flawed and corrupted, they make their way through life marked with a brokenness they can neither hide nor deny. But this does not mean they are without hope. It only means they depend on a deliverance they cannot offer themselves.

In this chapter we shall plot the destiny of these afflicted ones by focusing on Scobie, a police officer in the colony and the main character of the novel. *The Heart of the Matter* tells the story of this man who investigates the wayward, but himself becomes one of the strayed. He takes his own journey into darkness but in doing so reveals our greatest hope, namely, that we are held tight by a merciful love that is stronger than all our failings and deeper than all our faults. Scobie's journey is every person's journey and if his odyssey unmasks his deep corruption, it also lifts up a life-saving truth: a God who is love does not want anyone to be lost. In this chapter we shall develop this theme by examining three points: (1) why the human predicament is to be a fallen people in a fallen world; (2) why God's power is God's compassion; and (3) why a people who need to be rescued and redeemed must have a God whose love is greater than their failures. Hopefully, by exploring these issues we shall come to see "the heart of the matter."

Why All Is Not Well with Us as Fallen People in a Fallen World

In *The Heart of the Matter* Graham Greene peers into the depths of our human nature in order to see there the full truth of who we are. There is a theological anthropology at work throughout this novel and it is this: Human beings may be good, but all is not well with us. It is not only that much is missing to our wholeness and completion, but, more seriously, that we are stricken creatures in a stricken world. To know ourselves truthfully we have to acknowledge our kinship with the wayward as well as our fellowship in grace. Greene's gift is to show us that despite our achievements in goodness and our undeniable works of love, none of us is innocent and none is without guilt. Like everyone who has ever lived, we have done our share of evil.

This comes through the first time Scobie appears in the novel. We meet him driving up James Street past the Secretariat, the building which houses the administrative offices for the colony. The place reminds Scobie of a hospital and all who work there as patients, a metaphor which suggests not wellness but infirmity. Near the Secretariat is the building which houses the police station, the law courts, and the jail cells, the last of which takes up the largest area of the building. Behind the majesty and order of the courts lies the muck and squalor of the prison, home for those whose failures cannot be concealed. And the fact that those who transgressed the law stand side-by-side those paid to enforce it is Greene's way of saying we are all members of the same fallen household. It is not only the prisoners who need to be healed and rehabilitated, but the judges, lawyers, and police as well. Their corruption may not be as visible, but it is there. Even the best of us can make God weep through our petty thoughtlessness and everyday selfishness.

What It Means to Live after the Fall

The Heart of the Matter offers a literary parallel to the theological doctrine of original sin, a teaching which asserts that even though human beings "are good in important ways," we "are not *sound.*"[4] Both truths have to be kept in mind in order fully to understand who we are. Yes, we are God's very image and we can transcend ourselves in goodness and love, making others' lives indelibly better; however, we are also transgressors who find in ourselves a deep and pervasive propensity to evil that, left to ourselves, we cannot possibly overcome. *All is not well with us.* Contradictions flourish in our lives. We are well aware of our patterns of destructiveness, but knowing them does not stop us from embracing them. On a single day we can do something noble and beautifully good, but we can also be petty and mean, a fact which reminds us that there is in each of us something that is broken and undeniably flawed. Nothing in us is quite as it should be and we know this every time we hurt the ones we most want to love and every time we allow our best self to be lost.

The doctrine of original sin lets us in on a disturbing truth: before we do anything we are already broken. In the words of Psalm 51, "Indeed, I was born guilty, a sinner when my mother conceived me." We are *born off center,* born more than slightly skewed, and we continue to live off balance, which explains why we inevitably fall and why we find ourselves irresistibly attracted to behavior we know is not good for us. No matter how hard we try, we cannot keep our balance, and so we find ourselves falling into one mess after another. None of us has to live long before we realize our nature is seriously disordered in all its dimensions.

The purpose of the teaching of original sin is not to make us feel gloomy and hopeless about ourselves and the rest of humanity; rather it is to help us make sense of ourselves and the actual world in which we live, and in light of this to understand precisely the reason for our hope. In other words, we only understand the depth of our fallenness and the seriousness of our predicament because we have first glimpsed the glory possible for us. We are only able to deal squarely and seriously with our brokenness and our own responsibility in the proliferation of evil when we are first vividly aware of the freedom and forgiveness offered us in the death and resurrection of Christ. As James Alison makes eloquently clear, "the doctrine of original sin is not prior to, but follows from and is utterly dependent on, Jesus' resurrection from the dead and thus cannot be understood at all except in the light of that event."[5] In other words, Easter comes first, our fall from grace second. This is not our usual way of telling the story of salvation, but it is true inasmuch as it is only in light of Easter — only in light of Jesus' victory over sin and death — that we receive the hope and illumination necessary to grasp how profoundly and inescapably we are, without God's help, beings-unto-death. It is the Easter feast which discloses both the reasons for our hope and the depth of our predicament.

One of the best treatments of original sin comes from the medieval theologian Thomas Aquinas. Aquinas described original sin as a "bent towards disorder" that lives at the very center of who we are and effects every aspect and dimension of our lives.[6] Is there a more accurate description of ourselves than this? Is it not true that all of us wrestle with a "bent towards disorder" as long as we live? And is not this bent almost like a gravitational pull, luring us off center no matter how hard we try to resist it? We see the power of this disorder in our world, in our culture and society, in our families and relationships, and certainly in ourselves. It asserts itself in every lie, in every broken promise, in tidbits of malicious gossip, and in the global disorders that continue to beset us: poverty, oppression, torture, ecological devastation, violence, and, of course, war, which is the most flagrant and destructive manifestation of humanity's "bent towards disorder."

Original sin describes a disordered self and a disordered world. Our attitudes can be disordered, our values and perceptions, and certainly our actions. And for Aquinas this disorder is neither superficial nor partial; on the contrary, it is a malignancy of the spirit, a disintegrating force, which reaches into every dimension of ourselves and our world. Sometimes Aquinas captures this by describing original sin as a "congenital defect" of our nature, an illness and affliction which may not destroy us but which does leave us weakened and infirm.[7] Elsewhere, and perhaps more tellingly, he speaks of original sin as a complete wounding of our nature, a wounding that impairs our capacity to desire and to know the truth, our capacity to know, love, and embrace the good, and our capacity to deal with temptation and all the other wayward impulses of our lives.[8]

A Case of Mistaken Identity

Strangely enough, original sin is a doctrine of hope, not doom. It takes our waywardness seriously but only because it recognizes the true grace and promise of our lives. The core truth about humanity is not our depravity or our expertise in wickedness, but that we are essentially *religious creatures* called to friendship and communion with God and one another. If, as we noted above, Christianity starts with Easter, this means our fundamental identity is not as the fallen but as the forgiven. It is because we are forgiven that we can be more than fallen, because our lives originate in merciful grace, not corruption, that holiness is our truest self and everything else a case of mistaken identity. Sin may be real and its entanglements inescapable, but in every case sin represents our false identity; thus, if Easter means we are raised up in forgiveness and mercy to love and to enjoy God, and celebrates this as our truest identity and our most perfecting activity, to sin is to forget who we are and what God's grace both enables and summons us to be.

Greene captures this beautifully in a scene between Scobie and the captain of a Portuguese ship that has arrived in the colony. The time is the Second World War, and Scobie is sent on board the ship to search for possible contraband. In his search he discovers some letters hidden in the bathroom of the captain's quarters, one of them written from the captain to his daughter. Scobie opens the letter and reads:

> My dear, I am growing old, and after every voyage I am fatter: I am not a good man, and sometimes I fear that my soul in all this hulk of flesh is no larger than a pea. You do not know how easy it is for a man like me to commit the unforgivable despair. Then I think of my daughter. There was just enough good in me once for you to be fashioned. A wife shares too much of a man's sin

for perfect love. But a daughter may save him at the last. Pray for me, little spider. Your father who loves you more than life.[9]

The captain is keenly aware of his fallenness; and yet no matter how small the goodness he sees in himself, he clings to it as his only real hope, thinking it must count for something against all his failures. Buried underneath layers of corruption and lost possibilities, he spies a single but powerful glimmer of goodness in the love it took to bring his daughter to life and hopes that goodness is enough to save him.

What is going on here? The captain is much more aware of his failures than his goodness, but he nonetheless recognizes in that goodness his truest and most promising self. No matter how far he may have strayed from it, he knows it is who he ought to be and who he can be, and even though he reads the bulk of his life as a chronicle of mistakes and misgivings, because that spark of goodness still burns in him he sees all his errors as defections, each a falling away from what God's mercy and love have called him to be.

The captain's nostalgia for a goodness that once got the best of him and brought something beautiful to life reminds us that there is a power and resilience to goodness — even the smallest act of goodness — that no amount of accumulated evil can overcome. Like the captain, we can sometimes feel whatever goodness we may have achieved in our lives lies buried beneath layers of failures and regrets, but Greene's point (and Christianity's too) is that such goodness can never be extinguished. It lives on in us and in those it has touched, and the fact that we mourn our distance from it now testifies that it is in goodness, not evil, that we encounter our true selves and discover what God's forgiveness both calls and enables us to be.

But we cannot recover our true self until we first reckon with the self we have lost. One of the great paradoxes of Christianity seen in every story of every saint is that we do not begin our ascent to glory until we have first descended into the darkness of our hearts. We do not know what it is like to live in the freedom of grace until we first know what it is like to live in the slavery of sin. This is dramatic language but it fits; indeed, what Greene wants to show, principally through Scobie, is that the real drama of every human life is the drama of salvation, the story of our fall into darkness, our skill with habits of destructiveness, our

need for ongoing healing and regeneration, and our final and absolute
dependence on a merciful and forgiving love that can never be merited
but must be received as gift.

But we only know what it means to live from mercy when we have
first come face-to-face with our fallenness. For Greene, it is not just
that everyone falls, but that *everyone has to fall* — to bottom out in
helplessness — before they can be lifted up in grace and live from a
power that is not their own. Postures and pretensions are pointless. Illusions of self-sufficiency and well-being are a waste of time. Human
beings are masters of illusion, especially when it comes to denying
our transgressions and minimizing our brokenness. But self-deception
only worsens our predicament because it deprives us of what we need
to know and to see if we are to live not in illusion but in hope. Put
differently, we need true knowledge of ourselves, not just knowledge
that flatters, if we are ever to be more than beings-unto-death. Salvation begins when our illusions of well-being and self-sufficiency are
stripped away and in our nakedness we realize our absolute dependence
and our absolute need. But for most of us this happens only when we
have first lost our way in the beguiling labyrinth of sin.

A Nighttime Journey into Sin

In *The Heart of the Matter* Green illustrates this through Wilson's
nighttime journey to the bordello. His journey to the prostitutes becomes for Wilson a rite of passage, a sad initiation into his fellowship
with the fallen. As Greene tells the story, he offers a powerful analysis of the experience of sin. Wilson is drawn to the bordello almost
in spite of himself. Half from curiosity, half from lust, he sets out
that rainy evening not realizing he is about to encounter a part of his
humanity he had long denied having. The man who used to sneer at
the weaknesses of those walking to the bordello now takes that journey himself. Wilson knows what he is doing in surrendering to the
intoxicating appeal of temptation. He is no innocent victim for he lets
himself be lured, but as he goes he knows when the night is over he
will regret what he has done and will feel not contentment but shame.
Even before he sins he realizes what he is about to do makes no sense,

but it is as if he has peered so long over the precipice he cannot help but jump.

But Greene, while not denying Wilson's responsibility, also suggests that the bent towards disorder works so deeply and powerfully within us that it inevitably wins the day. Fallenness is too much part of who we are to escape its grip completely, and eventually it asserts its power over us, letting us know there is something at work in each of us that is stronger than our reason and our will. We see this in Wilson. Wilson knows where lust is leading him and he recognizes the essential irrationality in what he is about to undertake; but it is as if he must give this wayward part of himself its due. Peering over the precipice, almost hypnotized with danger, Wilson's fall from illusory innocence is the homage he must pay to his inherent corruption. In Wilson's nighttime visit to the prostitute, Greene presents the dichotomy at the heart of every transgression. Wilson knows well what is happening, and he also knows he can choose to reverse what he himself has begun; however, it is also true that his acquiescence to temptation is a surrender to forces and tendencies so deep in human nature that it is hard, even for the virtuous, to resist them.

We see this by dissecting Wilson's sin. As Greene tells the story two things are clear. First, Wilson has a choice. He is a free moral agent who is responsible for his actions. Second, it is equally clear that despite Wilson's freedom and responsibility, his own fall from grace illustrates that sometimes we are nearly victimized by the chaos and contradictions in our nature that draw us into situations we know will do us harm. We are accountable, but waywardness is so endemic to who we are that sometimes it seems impossible not to fall; indeed, if we are born and live "off balance," eventually this will manifest itself in our actions. We cannot walk off balance for long without falling. And so as Wilson makes his way to the prostitutes it is as if the brokenness of his nature has finally caught up with him. There is more a sense of sad resignation than heightened pleasure in what he is about to do. Greene presents the scene as a ritual of corruption through which every human being must pass. Wilson's nighttime journey is his walk into a darkness that captures us all.

What is odd about Wilson's lapse is that he knows his visit to the prostitute will not make him happy; in fact, he senses the sorrow and shame he will later feel before he crosses the threshold of the bordello: "He thought sadly, as lust won the day, what a lot of trouble it was; the sadness of the after-taste fell upon his spirits beforehand."[10] Still, something lures him on. Knowing the disgust and degradation that await him, he cannot turn back. Wilson is no different from the rest of humanity. Everyone falls and so must he. As he passes from temptation to enticement, from reluctance to surrender, and from surrender to shame, he knows he will not find in sin whatever happiness is missing from his life. Nevertheless, Wilson does what all of us so often do: he lets himself be captured.

> He felt an awful disappointment, as though he had not found what he was looking for.... What a fool I was, what a fool, to drive all the way for only this. The girl giggled as if she understood his stupidity.... [T]he way was blocked by an old mammy carrying a striped umbrella. She said something to the girl in her native tongue and received a grinning explanation. He had the sense that all this was only strange to *him,* that it was one of the stock situations the old woman was accustomed to meet in the dark regions which she ruled.[11]

A Revealing Sin of Omission and an Unexpected Sign of Hope

But Wilson is not the only one who falls. Scobie, too, encounters his corruption. It happens in this way. While Scobie's wife, Louise, is away from the colony, Scobie has a brief affair with Helen Rolt, a younger woman who survived a shipwreck off the shores of the colony. Ali, Scobie's faithful servant for fifteen years, discovers the affair, and Scobie, who never before has doubted Ali's trustworthiness, now wonders if he might betray him. And so Scobie goes to Yusef, the Syrian trader who has always told Scobie he would like to do a favor for him, and tells Yusef he is not sure he can trust Ali any longer. Yusef tells Scobie not to worry, he will take care of everything. Yusef takes care of everything by having Ali murdered.

Ironically this happens on November 1, Feast of All Saints. A day that began with Scobie going to mass to receive communion ends with him sitting quietly as Ali is murdered. Thinking of the feast which symbolizes, for Christians, the utmost glory and perfection of our humanity, Scobie wonders if he has fallen so far from who he could be that he is totally beyond redemption. He speaks of his heart as a hardened fossil, something grown so stony and decrepit nothing good could penetrate it, nothing hopeful reach it. He says to Yusef, "I've lost my way"[12] and reflects "that he had no shape left, nothing you could touch and say: this is Scobie."[13] It is as if Scobie despairs of ever finding his way back to his graced self. He feels broken beyond repair, lost to himself and lost to God. "It seemed to him," Greene writes, "that he had rotted so far that it was useless to make any effort. God was lodged in his body and his body was corrupting outwards from that seed."[14] And so there are two mortal wounds in this scene, one to Ali's body, the other to Scobie's soul. As Scobie looks down at Ali's bloodied body, he feels three things have been lost. He knows he has lost Ali, his trusted friend and companion; he feels he has lost himself; and he is sure he has lost God.

> Scobie thought: if only I could weep, if only I could feel pain; have I really become so evil? Unwillingly he looked down at the body. . . . Oh God, he thought, I've killed you: you've served me all these years and I've killed you at the end of them. God lay there under the petrol drums and Scobie felt the tears in his mouth, salt in the cracks of his lips. You served me and I did this to you. You were faithful to me, and I wouldn't trust you.
>   "What is it, sah?" the corporal whispered, kneeling by the body.
>   "I loved him," Scobie said.[15]

Is Scobie without hope? Even though the only thing he feels at the moment is the depth of his evil and the wretchedness of his sin, he forgets that he carries in his pocket a tiny medal of "a very obscure saint" given him in gratitude by the Portuguese captain whose smuggled letters Scobie did not report.

Scobie keeps this medal in his pocket until the end of the novel. It is a small but important reminder not only of a better self he has lost, but also of a hope that can never be taken away from him no matter how far he falls from grace. The medal of an "obscure saint" whose name no one remembers is a metaphor for Scobie's condition as well as our own. Greene suggests this man who rightly sees his corruption and guilt is also a man in whom grace continues to live, and a man who, despite undeniable sinfulness, is nonetheless called to, and capable of, holiness. The tiny medal is a reminder of a hope which outlasts even our most horrifying failures and sign of a call to sanctity even the worst of evils cannot extinguish. It is as if the tiny medal calls to him, "This is who you really are and no matter how far you stray you can always return to this truth." Greene's point is that in the end all that matters in the story of a human life is the goodness and holiness that shines in us; in Christian language, all that matters is that we become saints and that, Greene insists, is a hope we can never lose.

But why? The answer to this question comes from Scobie's second reason for hope. It is clear Greene does not believe we are the reason for our hope or that we can ever be the principal agents of our own regeneration. If rebirth, change, and renewal are always possibilities for us, from whence do they come? Greene's answer, of course, is from God. In the end, Greene insists, everyone is saved not by her or his goodness or virtue, but by a God who never gives up on us and a God whose love refuses to let us be lost. We see this vividly with Scobie; in fact, the very thing Scobie thinks will certainly damn him is the only thing that can possibly save him.

How so? Scobie is a Catholic and he has committed adultery with Helen Rolt. In the eyes of the church that is a serious sin, and Scobie, the church teaches, should not receive communion until he goes to confession and has his sin forgiven. But Scobie cannot have his sin forgiven unless he honestly tries to amend his life by ending his relationship with Helen Rolt, and that is something Scobie cannot promise. At the same time, if he goes to mass with his wife, Louise, but does not receive communion, she might be suspicious. The first time they attend mass Scobie is able to avoid receiving communion because shortly before Louise and he left home he broke his communion fast by sipping a little brandy. Scobie feels relief at this, a temporary reprieve, but he knows he cannot avoid communion forever. Seeing Louise and the others approaching the altar rail, and seeing Fr. Rank coming to them "with God in his hands," Scobie thinks, "God has just escaped me, but will He always escape?"[16]

Scobie asks the wrong question. The question is not if God will always escape Scobie, but will Scobie always escape God? The answer, of course, is no. Scobie's hope lies in the fact that he cannot ultimately escape God. He may flee from God and fall away from God and think he is forever lost to God, but Scobie cannot finally lose God because God will not allow Scobie to be lost. And the reason is that in God we find a love none of our failures can conquer, none of our transgressions destroy.

Greene suggests this the next time Scobie goes to church with Louise and has no reason not to receive communion. Watching "the priest pour the wine and water into the chalice," Scobie felt "his own damnation" was "being prepared like a meal at the altar."[17] And when he kneels alongside Louise at the communion rail, waiting for Fr. Rank to come to him with the body of Christ, Scobie thinks "only a miracle can save me now."[18]

Scobie speaks the truth in ways he does not understand. He feels he has fallen beyond the pale of grace, he is convinced he lives forever outside the love and mercy of God; and yet the truth is not only that a miracle *can save him,* but *that it will save him,* and what is true for Scobie is true for all of us. All of us are saved by a miracle. All of us have hope only because of a miracle. It is the miracle of God's love, the miracle of God's absolute forgiveness, the miracle of God's gracious patience and indefatigable fidelity. Scobie is not the only one who depends on the power of a miracle. All of us do. We live in grace and goodness and hope only because we live from a love that refuses to give up on us, a love that refuses to let go, a love that refuses to take all our refusals as final. Scobie misses this because he is so convinced he is falling into a darkness that can never end that he never stops to think that God might be reaching out for him with a love no darkness can shatter.

Nonetheless, Scobie came close to "the heart of the matter" on his earlier visit to church with Louise. Watching her go to communion, Scobie reflects on the extremes to which God goes to love us and to reach us. He thinks of God reaching out to us, seeking us and wanting to be with us, when in Jesus God became a Palestinian Jew and walked our dusty earth. He thinks of how today God continues to reach out to us when throughout the world God becomes present to us in the bread and wine of the eucharist. Scobie thinks of how "desperately God must love,"[19] of how passionately committed God must be in wanting to love us and to be with us. In other words, what Greene suggests through Scobie's reverie is that the real "heart of the matter" has absolutely nothing to do with our own fallenness and brokenness and sinfulness, but absolutely everything to do with the goodness and mercy of God.

Why God's Power Is God's Compassion

And so what kind of God do we have? Do we have a God worthy of worship? *The Heart of the Matter* not only probes the human soul, it also probes the heart and soul of God and, through the character of Scobie, raises questions about the character of God. Greene suggests we cannot know the heart and soul of God without reckoning with suffering, which is precisely the human experience that can most make us question God. But Greene pushes us to see that to know God truly we must plumb the darkness of suffering because it is there in the abyss that we encounter not the absence of God or the heartless indifference of God but the compassionate presence of God. In other words, *The Heart of the Matter* suggests it is in suffering that we not only can be most intimately united with God, but can also come to the most exquisite and profound knowledge of God.

Book Two of the novel opens with the story of some survivors of a shipwreck who come to the colony after having spent forty days on the open sea in lifeboats. Most of the passengers died during those forty days, and the few who survived are barely clinging to life. Two of those survivors catch Scobie's attention, Helen Rolt, a nineteen-year-old woman whose husband did not survive (it is with her Scobie has an affair), and a young girl, about six years old, whose barely lived life is slipping away.

Scobie is drawn into the young girl's suffering, and it makes him question God. Suffering almost always raises questions about God because it is hard to reconcile our beliefs about the perfect goodness and love of God with the unexplainable and incomprehensible evil we encounter in the suffering of the innocent, especially the suffering of children. Why doesn't God intervene? Why does not a God who is supposed to be love itself *do something?* If the God of the universe is powerful enough to create everything that is, should not this God use an eyeblink of his power to ease the suffering of a powerless child? We always say God is infinitely greater than us, but a God who seems unmoved by the tears of the world seems less than human and certainly less moral than us; after all, which one of us wouldn't do everything possible to ease the suffering of a child? If we, with all our faults and imperfections, would reach out in love to a suffering child, why should we worship a God who seems to do nothing? There is no way we can or should ever say such suffering is good or serves some higher purpose. It is evil and it ought to make us question the God we are summoned to love.

What Should We Do When God Seems to Do Nothing?

But sometimes there are no answers to the questions for which we most need answers. Suffering raises basic questions about the nature and character of God: Is God truly good? Is God really powerful? How can God love us when so many in our world are suffering? But more often than not we must live without answers. We have no explanation. Certainty eludes us. And when people try to give us answers we find them unconvincing. When it comes to reconciling the evil of suffering with the goodness of God, most of us are at a loss. Suffering is the great unanswered question; like God, it is one mystery we never completely penetrate.[20]

Nonetheless, perhaps the mystery of suffering is illuminated not in speculation but in love. Scobie has no answer to why God allows the young girl to suffer, but having no answer to suffering does not mean there is nothing he can do in the face of suffering. Put differently, if God's love seems absent at this moment, it does not mean Scobie's love must be absent as well.

Scobie sits with the little girl as she lies dying. This is not easy for him because it reminds him of the death of his own daughter, Catherine, several years earlier, a death he was not present to witness. Scobie was relieved to have missed his daughter's death because it saved him from having to watch her suffer. Now he sits watching a stranger suffer and finds her agony so unbearable that he wants to flee.

However, he stays, and it is compassion that keeps him there. As Scobie keeps vigil with the dying child, he is drawn into her affliction and begins to pray. When he says, "Father, look after her. Give her peace.... Take away my peace for ever, but give her peace,"[21] the little girl, slipping in and out of consciousness, thinks that Scobie is her father. As she lies there dying, each breath growing more labored than the one before, she whispers, "Father," and instead of denying that he is her father, Scobie responds, "Yes, dear. Don't speak, I'm here."[22] In the last moments of this little girl's life, Scobie gives her comfort by letting her believe someone who loves her is with her.

Maybe what Greene suggests here is that our most fitting response to the sorrow and suffering of the world is to be with those who suffer and to do whatever we can to lighten their burden and ease their pain. Maybe what we are called to do before all the tears and grief and affliction of the world is *to risk compassion* by opening ourselves to the sufferings of others and entering into them lest they be left to suffer alone. This is what Scobie does when he keeps vigil with the dying child. His strongest instinct is to flee her sufferings because he knows if he stays he will suffer too. His urge is to leave the dying child to suffer alone because there is no way he can be present without being drawn into her affliction. But his compassion is stronger than his fear, and in the last seconds of her life he so completely joins his life to hers that he becomes her father and she, no longer stranger, becomes his little girl. Through his compassion the little girl dies loved instead of alone.

Is this too "the heart of the matter"? In a world of so much suffering and grief and sorrow and affliction, is "the heart of the matter" our willingness to stand with those who suffer instead of abandoning them? Confronted with the anguish and pain and tears of so many, are we called to risk compassion? Perhaps the "heart of the matter" is to realize that even though we may not always have power to take away a person's sorrow or to ease their sufferings, we do have a different kind of power, namely, the power to be with them in their suffering and to keep vigil with them in their pain even when doing so brings pain and suffering to us.

This is the power of compassion. The human instinct is to flee suffering, not share in it. Compassion is the virtue that transcends instinct because when confronted with the agony of another the person of compassion does not flee their suffering, but partakes in it so that those who suffer never have to suffer alone. What Greene shows through Scobie is that our power may not lie in *removing* suffering but *sharing in it*. In one obvious sense Scobie is powerless because there was nothing he could do to save the dying child's life; his power did not lie there. But what he could do is be present to the dying child and through his presence join his life to hers precisely in her sufferings. Love always brings union, and compassion is the love that unites us with others in their sufferings. There may be no riskier or more costly love than compassion, but in a world of sorrow and tears there is no more urgent expression of love. In the face of unmovable suffering, it may be the only power we have.

Finding God in the Wounds of the World

Do we then overcome the absence of God by the presence of our own compassion? Some, like the French existentialist Albert Camus, have thought so; but in *The Heart of the Matter* Greene pushes us to question the assumption that suffering spells the absence of God by suggesting it reveals the most intense manifestation of the presence of God. This can happen in two ways. First, God can be present to those who suffer through the power of our own compassion. Christians have always believed that God works through us to achieve good things; this is why every Christian is challenged to mediate the presence of God in his or her life. God is love, mercy, faithfulness, justice, and forgiveness, but we come to know each of these qualities of God when we experience them through one another. Thus, when Scobie shows compassionate love for the dying girl it does not mean that God fails to love, but that God loves through Scobie's love; similarly, it does not mean God is not present to her sufferings, but that God is present through Scobie's compassion.

God's love is always an embodied love. It was embodied foremost and definitively in Jesus, but it is also truly embodied in each of us whenever we dare emulate the love and goodness of God. Part of the beauty and humility of God is that God chooses to do good through us; indeed, we can even say God depends on us inasmuch as God wants us to be instruments of providence and agents of grace. In other words, God is limited only to the degree that we refuse to use the gift of our freedom at the service of love.

But suffering can reveal the presence of God in a second way. Suffering may raise questions about the love and goodness of God, and when we suffer we may, like the crucified Christ, feel we have been abandoned by God; and yet the most powerful message of the Cross is that God is not only present to us in our sufferings but shares in them. If we take the incarnation of God in Christ seriously and understand it in its most radical implications, we see that in Christ God enters into every dimension of our humanity, including our sufferings. The absolute surrender of God to our humanity is most vividly displayed in the crucified Christ because the Cross shows that God does not flee the sorrow and pain of our world but enters into it, shares it, and at every moment is deeply a part of it. The Cross tells us that the God of the universe is not distant and disengaged from our world and our lives; rather, God is a fellow-sufferer, supreme in pathos and sympathy. What the Cross testifies is that God makes our sufferings his own.[23]

This is hard for us to grasp because we do not think of the God of the universe, a God we claim as perfect and all-powerful, as capable of suffering. We picture God as so far removed from the world and our everyday lives that we cannot imagine God being affected by anything that happens to us. But the Cross of Christ says otherwise. The Cross suggests God is most completely revealed in the sufferings of Christ and continues to be present *in suffering* wherever there are crucified in our world. God is there in the cross of the poor, in the cross of the violated and abused, in the cross of the homeless and downtrodden, in the cross of victims of hatred and discrimination, and in the cross of the sufferings of the innocent. Christians have always believed that in their sufferings they participate in the sufferings of the crucified Christ; but there is a second message in the Cross and it is that through the Cross God participates in our sufferings as well. The word of the Cross is this: Our passion is God's passion. When we suffer, God suffers with us. More than anything, what the life, ministry, passion, and death of

Jesus witness is that God does not flee the world's suffering but makes our suffering his own.

There is a scene in *The Heart of the Matter* which suggests this. At dinner one evening a group of British officials in the colony are discussing the suicide of Pemberton, one of their colleagues. They speak so casually of Pemberton's suicide that Scobie thinks to himself, "Through two thousand years ... we have discussed Christ's agony in just this disinterested way."[24] Scobie's reflection hints that the suffering of Christ did not end on the Cross, but continues wherever there is anguish, sorrow, suffering, and distress in the world today. The passion of Christ was not a single, isolated event but is ongoing and unfinished; indeed, it lives not only in the violent death of the Son of God, but in all the violence, bloodshed, murder, and abuse that continues to scar our world.

Finding Compassion as Power

How does this relate to the death of the little girl? What do her sufferings reveal about God? If the Cross tells us we are to look for God not foremost in the glamour and splendor of the world but in its sufferings, then God was not only present to that dying child but was suffering and dying with her. Maybe the reason we sometimes feel the absence of God in our sufferings is that we are not accustomed to looking for God there; we do not expect to find God in our sorrow and pain. But the Cross is God's way of saying, "This is where you are to find me, this is where you are to look for me." Suffering is where we can be sure of God's presence not because God approves of our suffering, but because God loves us enough to share in our suffering.

And that is compassion. If Scobie's power lay not in removing the little girl's suffering but in sharing in it, the Cross suggests it is no different with God. God's power is God's compassion, God's unsurpassable vulnerability to the wounds and brokenness of our world.[25] All this is quite scandalous because we are not sure we want to worship a God who enters the world not through the triumphs of the conquerors but through the wounds of the broken and defeated. Worshiping a whipped and wounded God is not something we readily embrace because it challenges so many of our ideas about greatness and power. If

God's power is God's compassion, then God's omnipotence cannot be measured by God's capacity to take away our sufferings, but by God's absolute willingness to enter fully into them and to make our sufferings God's own. In short, we will be frustrated if we look to God to find an answer to our sufferings because, as Nicholas Wolterstorff observes, "Instead of explaining our suffering God shares it."[26]

And so here we see the upside down ways of God. The Cross shouts that God's power thrives in what to us seems like weakness and defeat. The Cross shouts that God's power is not the power to control or determine or always to conquer; rather, God's power is the power of suffering love. The Judeo-Christian tradition has consistently defined the very essence of God as love, but the Cross further articulates the nature of God's love by suggesting that God is not just love, but is *essentially suffering love.* God suffers not because God is weak and defeated, but precisely because God is absolute and unconditional love; indeed, God's sufferings are unlimited because God's love is unlimited. Like Scobie with the dying girl, a God who is truly love willingly shares in every moment of the lives of those God loves, including their sufferings.

Can it really be any other way? Classically, theologians have described God as unchanging, immovable, utterly self-sufficient, and incapable of being affected or influenced by anything. But the God defined through the categories of classical Greek philosophy is not the God we encounter in the Bible and surely not the God unveiled on the Cross.[27] And is a God who cannot be touched by the sufferings and afflictions of our world worthy of glory and praise? Is not a God void of compassion and suffering love actually more demonic than divine?[28] The Cross revolutionizes our image of God and challenges all our thinking about God but ultimately presents us with the only hopeful understanding of God because the Cross reveals that we have a crucified God, and a crucified God finally overcomes all the grief and tears of the world through the meek yet unassailable power of compassion; and, as the resurrection indicates, the great Christian paradox is that compassion — God's suffering love — is finally more powerful than death.

If we return to the scene of Scobie's anguished vigil with the dying girl, we are able to interpret it in a new way. Now we see that Scobie's compassion was not a replacement for God but the most fitting way for him to image and imitate God. If the essence of God is compassionate, suffering love, then we who are God's images most keenly reveal God when we risk compassion for those who suffer.[29] And as God's images we are called to make God's power our own. This is not easy because compassion demands that we, like Scobie, make our hearts available to another's pain. Compassion is a hard power to live by precisely because of the vulnerability to suffering it requires. A compassionate person is no stranger to pain; quite the opposite, we have the virtue of compassion only when our hearts have been pierced by sharing in another's sorrow.

But what we also see is that Scobie's compassion does not rival or even parallel God's but is united to it. When we love, our love is joined to the love of God, and this is true whether love takes the form of affection, delight, affirmation, mercy, or compassion. God and humanity come together in love, and this is also true in suffering love. When in our compassion we participate in the suffering of another, we are one with the compassion of God. In compassion God and humanity come together; more strongly put, through compassion God and humanity *suffer together.* In the suffering of the dying girl Scobie may not have perceived the presence of God because what he failed to realize is that God was present to her by being one with him in his own suffering love. Nicholas Wolterstorff captures this perfectly when he writes, "We're in it together, God and we, together in the history of our world. The history of our world is the history of our suffering together."[30]

Why We Need a God
Who Is Greater Than Our Failures

The last part of *The Heart of the Matter* focuses on Scobie and his growing despair. A Catholic, Scobie believes his love for Helen Rolt has imperiled his soul, but it is a love he cannot renounce. He knows what the church teaches, that he should confess his sin, amend his life, do penance for his misguided love with Helen, and, with a repentant spirit, deepen his love for his wife, Louise. But love creates ties and brings responsibilities, and love, Scobie thinks, has bound him both to Louise and to Helen. He cannot desert those he has promised to love without being guilty of unfaithfulness; but if he continues in his love for Helen he not only betrays Louise, but also betrays God. In the teaching of the church, Scobie, who has committed adultery, is in a state of mortal sin; thus, his love for Helen has not only damaged his relationship with his wife, but has also jeopardized his relationship with God. Indeed, Scobie believes his love for Helen damns him and that his refusal to repent separates him from God forever.

And so Scobie, confronted by the entanglements of incompatible loves, despairs, and in the last pages of the novel he, the policeman who has been trained to detect crimes, plans "the worst crime a Catholic could commit."[31] He plots his own death, and like any killer trying to cover his tracks, Scobie schemes to make it appear that he died from problems of the heart — angina — and not by taking his life.

A few days before he plans to kill himself, Scobie sits in the back of a church and talks to God about what he has decided to do. In his monologue to God, Scobie tells God that just as Louise and Helen will be better off when he takes his life and frees them of him forever, God will be better off too. Sitting there in the darkness of the church, Scobie states his case:

> You'll be better off if you lose me once and for all. I know what I'm doing. I'm not pleading for mercy. I am going to damn myself, whatever that means. I've longed for peace and I'm never going to know peace again. But you'll be at peace when I am out of your reach. It will be no use then sweeping the floor to find me or searching for me over the mountains. You'll be able to forget me, God, for eternity.[32]

Is God Better Off without Us?

Can God forget us? Is God ever better off without us? Scobie's image of God "sweeping the floor" and "searching over the mountains" echoes two parables Jesus told to illustrate the impassioned relentlessness of

God's love. They are in the fifteenth chapter of the Gospel of Luke and both underscore the extremes to which God goes in search of those who are lost. The first is the story of the shepherd who has a hundred sheep. One wanders away and the shepherd leaves the ninety-nine to search for the one that is lost, rejoicing when it is found. The second tells the story of a woman who has ten silver pieces but loses one. She sweeps every corner of her house in search of that coin, not able to rest until it is found, and celebrates with her friends and neighbors when that single silver piece is once more in her possession.

Such are the ways of God's love. If neither the shepherd nor the woman could be at peace until they found what they had lost, the same is true with God. Both parables depict the extremes to which God will go to make sure no one is ever finally lost to God's love. If we wander away from God, God will find us. If we despair of God's mercy, of hope and understanding, God's mercy will embrace us and God's hope will be ours because God never despairs of us.

And so even if we desert God, God will not desert us. And even when we, like Scobie, claim to be letting go of God, God cannot, finally, let go of us. And the reason is that God's mercy is always greater than our failures, God's love infinitely deeper than our despair. This comes through in Scobie's prayer. What begins as his final soliloquy — a last testament uttered from the abyss — becomes a saving grace, even though Scobie does not realize it is a grace he is meant to seize, a lifeline he should grasp. He sits in the church thinking he speaks to a silent God, a God who may hear but will never respond. But as Scobie explains why he must take his life, he hears another voice speaking from deep inside him, a voice of love, grief, and affection pleading from the center of his broken spirit. It is the voice of the love that made him, the voice of the love that knows him better than he knows himself, and it says to Scobie,

You say you love me, and yet you'll do this to me — rob me of you for ever. I made you with love. I've wept your tears. I've saved you from more than you will ever know; I planted in you this longing for peace only so that one day I could satisfy your longing and watch your happiness. And now you push me away, you put me out of your reach.[33]

How could God be relieved at Scobie's death? How could God possibly be better off losing a man God has created from love and has never failed to love? Sometimes we think God is perfectly happy regardless of what happens to us, but Greene suggests otherwise. Sometimes we think God loses nothing, suffers nothing, feels nothing, no matter what harm we bring to ourselves, but to believe this is to completely miss the point of God's love. If we cannot imagine our lives without the people we most love, neither can God. If we could not possibly be happy, satisfied, content, or at peace if certain people were forever lost to us, the same is true with a God who is mercy and affection and love through and through.

Think of the great extremes and endless transformations God has gone through to be part of our lives: taking on our flesh, walking in our world, sharing our joys and afflictions, reaching us through others. Would God go to such lengths to be with us if God could be God without us? And if it is the nature of a lover to want to be one with the beloved, could the perfect lover we call God accept permanent estrangement from any of the beloved? Would not that violate the very nature of God? Maybe "the heart of the matter" comes to this: God is in us and *we are in God*, and that means even if we do not always love well enough to know we need God, God needs and wants us. Perfect love can have it no other way.

The True Heart of the Matter

This is our hope and it is a hope which shines through the darkness of the last night of Scobie's life. He sits with his wife, Louise, knowing that as soon as she goes upstairs to bed he will swallow the rest of the pills and wait to die. Scobie realizes "everything he did now was for the last time," and that with every moment "the actions which could be repeated became fewer and fewer."[34] And so he talks with Louise, trying to extend the last moments of his life by keeping her with him as long as possible. And when Scobie can think of nothing else for them to talk about, he asks Louise to read to him. She reads a poem, but in his turmoil and distress the only thing Scobie hears are these lines:

> We are all falling. This hand's falling too —
> all have this falling sickness none withstands.

> And yet there's always One whose gentle hands
> this universal falling can't fall through.[35]

This indeed is "the heart of the matter," to be fallen yet embraced, to be misbegotten but perfectly loved. The message Greene proclaims throughout *The Heart of the Matter* is that to know ourselves we have to accept both truths: to be human is to have "this falling sickness," but it is also to know that when we fall, we fall not into an abyss of darkness and despair, but into the merciful love of God. Our hope, our salvation, our eternal reassurance is to know there is one love we cannot *fall through*, but will *fall into*, and that love is the divine compassion, the infinite mercy of a God who will never give up on us and who will never count us as lost. And so we can stumble, we can rebel, we can sin grievously, we can transgress and we can, like Scobie, even despair; but we do all these things rooted in grace and bound to a love we can never destroy.

Consider the way Scobie dies. Louise goes upstairs and Scobie swallows the pills. As he sits waiting to die he tries to make an act of contrition, but can get no further than the words, "I am sorry and beg pardon."[36] He begins to lose consciousness, but thinks he hears someone outside the house calling to him, someone in trouble or pain who needs his help and is trying to reach him. Getting up, now more in death than in life, Scobie stumbles toward the door and whispers, "Dear God, I love...,"[37] before death overtakes him. As he falls, the medal the Portuguese captain had given him, the medal of the "obscure saint" whose name no one could remember, rolls out of his pocket and slides across the floor.

Who was calling to him? Who was trying to reach him? Was it Helen Rolt, whom Scobie had tried to visit one final time earlier in the day? Was it Christ, whom Scobie was sure he had insulted and betrayed, and who, Scobie was convinced, would want nothing more to do with him? Could it have been both? And what do we make of Scobie's last words, "Dear God, I love...," a sentence he was unable to complete? How would Scobie have finished the sentence? To whom was he professing his love: Louise? Helen? God?

In a way, it does not matter because ultimately what saves us are not our broken efforts at love, but God's love. The last word about us is not our sins and our transgressions, no matter how great they may be, but God's mercy. Greene suggests this in the final scene of the novel when Louise, fully aware of Scobie's affair with Helen Rolt, goes to Fr. Rank. She tells the weathered priest that Scobie was "a bad Catholic," to which the priest immediately replies, "That's the silliest phrase in common use."[38] She tells him there is no use praying for a man who has taken his own life because anyone who commits suicide places himself outside of God's mercy. Strangely, the usually unperturbable priest reacts to this vehemently, telling Louise,

"For goodness' sake, Mrs. Scobie, don't imagine you — or I — know a thing about God's mercy."

"The Church says..."

"I know the Church says. The Church knows all the rules. But it doesn't know what goes on in a single human heart."[39]

And sometimes it does not know what goes on in the heart of God. Earlier in the novel when Scobie first contemplated suicide he admitted that the church taught it "was the unforgivable sin, the final expression of an unrepentant despair." But he also recalled "that God had sometimes broken his own laws, and was it less possible for him to put out a hand of forgiveness into the suicidal darkness than to have woken himself in the tomb, behind the stone?"[40]

It is a fascinating insight. Greene suggests mercy and forgiveness always get the best of God, that in God mercy and forgiveness always triumph over condemnation. When it comes to God, love always wins out, mercy always conquers, and again it is the Cross which most eloquently reveals this. On the Cross God wears no disguises. Everything is stripped away and only love remains. And so when Greene says even God "had broken his own laws," perhaps what he means is that in God love always surpasses law; or, perhaps better, that the one law God will never break is the law of the Cross, the law of absolute, unconditional, merciful love.

It is in this truth that we find our freedom, in this truth that we never lose hope. Scobie's story is everyone's story. He is a flawed lover, a sometimes terribly wayward son, who depends on a deliverance he cannot offer himself. But it is a deliverance he has already received, a deliverance he can live from day after day and a deliverance on which he can always depend. And this is because the ultimate "heart of the matter" is that God is mercy through and through, that God is the compassion that never gives up on us, and that God is the love which refuses to let us be lost. Thus, even though Scobie and the rest of the castaways may be a long way from Eden, they may also be much closer than they think to the kingdom of God.

In this chapter we have presented a view of human beings and their world as seen through the lens of Christian theology. What is revealed there is both an unblinking acceptance of human corruption and a firm belief in our possibilities for goodness and love. In conversation with Graham Greene's *The Heart of the Matter*, we have seen that sometimes the only response both God and ourselves can give to suffering is the power of compassionate love. Most importantly, we learned that no matter how deep our flaws or how storied our waywardness, our hope lies precisely in the love we find in God, a love that is far stronger than our most momentous failures and more resilient than our sins. The following authors have also explored one or more of these themes, though some in ways quite different from Graham Greene.

Algren, Nelson, *The Man with the Golden Arm*
Banks, Russell, *Continental Drift*
Bernanos, Georges, *The Diary of a Country Priest*
Camus, Albert, *The Fall*
———, *The Plague*
Conrad, Joseph, *Heart of Darkness*
Davies, Robertson, *The Rebel Angels*
———, *What's Bred in the Bone*
Endu, Shusaku, *Silence*
Faulkner, William, *The Sound and the Fury*

Heaney, Seamus, *The Cure at Troy*
Hugo, Victor, *Les Misérables*
Kennedy, William, *Billy Phelan's Greatest Game*
McCullough, Colleen, *The Thorn Birds*
Miller, Arthur, *After the Fall*
O'Connor, Flannery, *A Good Man Is Hard to Find*
O'Neill, Eugene, *A Moon for the Misbegotten*
————, *Long Day's Journey into Night*
Steinbeck, John, *East of Eden*

Notes

1. Graham Greene, *The Heart of the Matter* (New York: Viking Penguin, 1971), 11. Subsequent page references to the novel refer to this a edition only. Different editions, of course, will have different page references. **2.** Greene, 13. **3.** Greene, 13.

4. Cornelius Plantinga, Jr., *Not the Way It's Supposed to Be: A Breviary of Sin* (Grand Rapids, Mich.: William B. Eerdmans, 1995), 33.

5. James Alison, *The Joy of Being Wrong: Original Sin through Easter Eyes* (New York: Crossroad, 1998), 3.

6. Thomas Aquinas, *Summa Theologiae* (New York: McGraw-Hill, 1969), I–II, 82,1. **7.** Ibid., 82,2. **8.** Ibid., 85,3.

9. Greene, 54. **10.** Greene, 173. **11.** Greene, 174. **12.** Greene, 245. **13.** Greene, 246. **14.** Greene, 244. **15.** Greene, 247–48. **16.** Greene, 213. **17.** Greene, 224. **18.** Greene, 225. **19.** Greene, 213.

20. For a superb reflection on these points see Nicholas Wolterstorff, *Lament for a Son* (Grand Rapids, Mich.: William B. Eerdmans, 1987).

21. Greene, 125. **22.** Greene, 125.

23. For further treatment of this point see Arthur C. McGill, *Suffering: A Test of Theological Method* (Philadelphia: Westminster Press, 1982).

24. Greene, 193.

25. A very fine explication of this point can be found in Sally B. Purvis, *The Power of the Cross: Foundations for a Christian Feminist Ethic of Community* (Nashville: Abingdon Press, 1993), especially pp. 69–81.

26. Wolterstorff, *Lament for a Son*, 81.

27. See Daniel Day Williams, *The Spirit and the Forms of Love* (New York: University Press of America, 1981), especially pp. 16–33.

28. See Elizabeth A. Johnson, *She Who Is: The Mystery of God in Feminist Theological Discourse* (New York: Crossroad, 1995), 246–72; Catherine Mowry LaCugna, *God for Us: The Trinity and Christian Life* (San Francisco: HarperCollins, 1991); Sallie McFague, *Models of God: Theology for an Ecological, Nuclear Age* (Philadelphia: Fortress Press, 1987).

29. Wolterstorff makes this point in *Lament for a Son,* 83. **30.** Ibid., 91.

31. Greene, 257. **32.** Greene, 258. **33.** Greene, 258. **34.** Greene, 262. **35.** Greene, 264. **36.** Greene, 265. **37.** Greene, 265. **38.** Greene, 271. **39.** Greene, 272. **40.** Greene, 190.

CHAPTER THREE

LOVE

Learning Its Limits and Lessons

B EWARE OF LOVES that soar too high. Christians are called to love
everybody, even our enemies, but we have to wonder if that is
healthy, even possible. Or we at least have to wonder how an enemy
is to be loved. We have all heard stories of loyal lovers who stood fast
during years of neglect, ridicule, and even abuse. They entered love
looking for life, but love cost them their lives. They did not emerge
from these relationships stronger, but beaten down and, sometimes, destroyed. Their lovers had become their enemies, stealing life when they
should have been giving it. Their love was patient, long-suffering, and
certainly faithful, but practicing those virtues in relationships where
there was much given but little received left them more dead than alive.

Love should not lead to our destruction. Even the martyrs saw their
deaths not as an end but as an absolute beginning; for them to die
was to gain fullness of life. Love ought to be a path to life, not diminishment and death. But to know this we must learn (and accept)
love's limits. There may not be limits to God's love, but there certainly
are limits to ours. To love rightly we must learn the limits of love,
and the most important first lesson in love's limits is to learn God can
love in ways we cannot. God may be able to love everybody perfectly
and personally, but our hearts are tied to time and place, and they are
certainly tied to some persons more than others.[1] There are limits in
ourselves and limits in the love we can give.

But there are also limits in the love we should give. If someone we
have long tried to love has made him- or herself more enemy than
friend, at the very least we should put some distance between that

person and ourselves. And if like Christ we try to love our enemies, we better have someone nearby who loves us truly as friend. It is better to practice the love we can give than to be destroyed by striving for a love we cannot. This sounds harsh and cynical for people schooled in the gospel where disciples are instructed to turn the other cheek and to suffer hostilities silently, but we need to accept the God-given limitations of our nature and, even more so, realize that even though Jesus summoned us to love our enemies, he never intended that to be the primary love of our lives. Enemies may be inevitable and we have to learn what it means to love them, but the heart of our love should be directed to those partners, family members, and friends who love us as we love them and, unlike our enemies, truly want what is best for us.

The danger of loves that soar too high is that unless they are pursued prudently and carefully they can, like wayward rockets, return to destroy us. God does not hold us to self-destructive loves, no one else should, and we should certainly not demand it of ourselves. One of the key challenges of the moral life is to learn the love we can and should give; or, to put it differently, to learn how we should order the various loves of our lives so that we know the difference between loving an enemy and loving a friend. When we do, we discover that even though sacrifice is part of any love, it is not, and never should be, the heart of love.

This is one of the lessons of Mary Gordon's *Final Payments,* a novel that explores the dangers of costly devotion.[2] It is the story of Isabel Moore, a young woman who for eleven years had made her invalid father's world her own. In caring every day for her father — bathing and dressing him, feeding him, sleeping when he slept — she had conformed the rhythms of her young life to his dying one. In doing so she gained the admiration of many, but sacrificed friendships, her youth, and almost any semblance of a normal life. Isabel did so because she loved her father intensely and believed, perhaps rightly, that she never would have such an all-consuming love again in her life. But her absolute devotion to her father mirrored her belief that the greatest loves are the most costly and that we are summoned to love most not those we know will faithfully love us in return, but precisely the ones whose love and affection we may never feel. For love to be real, Isabel thinks, it has to be sacrificial.

Can we pay too great a price for love? This is the question *Final Payments* asks. Through the story of Isabel Moore, Mary Gordon investigates the nature, and limits, of genuine love. How ought human beings love? Should we love everyone in exactly the same way? Should we love some more than others? And are there some loves of which we should be wary? Isabel is torn between believing, on the one hand, that the most perfect love is the most demanding one, and wanting, on the other hand, to love and be loved by one whose affection and devotion brings her life and joy.

The limits and lessons of love, this is what *Final Payments* is about. We shall explore Mary Gordon's treatment of the love which best befits us by considering four points: (1) the difference between love understood as sacrifice and love understood as mutual care and affection; (2) why love requires being special to somebody; (3) why love demands honesty about the needs and limits of our nature; and (4) why love is a matter of caring for, and being grateful for, a gift.

Why We Need to Understand the Difference between Love as Sacrifice and Love as Care

We meet Isabel Moore on the day of her father's funeral, a day which commemorated not only the end of his life, but the end of a definite period in Isabel's life as well. When Isabel was nineteen, her father suffered a stroke. For the next eleven years she gave her life for him, allowing his needs to govern her own. Isabel's routines were mapped by the demands of a slowly dying invalid: bringing him breakfast, shaving and bathing him, wheeling him to the table for lunch, shopping in the afternoon, preparing his dinner, going to bed early. Her life had shrunk to the size of her dying father's, her world becoming no bigger than his own. If paralysis confined him to their house in Queens, she limited herself to that world as well. Over the next eleven years Isabel absorbed the marks of the dying. "I am sure that for all the years I took care of my father I carried the smell of his sickness with me," she tells us, "a sour, male smell unnatural to me as a woman."[3]

Her father's sickness separated Isabel from the world that should have been her own. This woman who should have been moving into the prime of her life yoked herself to a man who was leaving it. It was not a natural thing for a nineteen-year-old to do, forsaking friends and activities and hopes and joys to "minister to the decay" of her father.[4] Isabel acknowledges that often during those eleven years when she abandoned her life to be with the dying, her friends urged her to get help, frightened to see what Isabel's decision was doing to her, arguing that no daughter's duties should exact such a cost. They watched in alarm as Isabel's devotion changed her in ways they found disturbing. They could not see why her commitment should be so all-consuming or why she viewed any deviation from routine as a failure in faithfulness, a selfish aberration. Thus, when Isabel declined a vacation with her friend, Eleanor, because her father pleaded, "Don't leave me," Eleanor told her, "You are letting him eat you alive."[5] Isabel did not disagree, but thought Eleanor missed the point. The question was not what her devotion was costing her, but what love demands.

Isabel may have loved her father more than anyone else, but it is not clear she loved him rightly. She gave her father absolute devotion, but that may have been a mistake because the love that kept her father alive left her slowly dying; it was as if there was one lifeline between them, but it flowed only one way. Isabel believed the most perfect love was selfless love, but as Mary Gordon illustrates, Isabel's willingness to sacrifice everything to care for her father may have been well-intended, but it was not wise because in practicing such love she had no life apart from her father's dying. Her selfless love obliterated her, slowing erasing the distinctive and most promising features of herself. Bit-by-bit, day-by-day, she disappeared into the devouring needs of her father. She abandoned outside interests, she seldom saw her friends, she resisted any opportunity to be drawn outside the world of the dying. In her absolute love for her father, Isabel disappeared as his deterioration became a metaphor of her own. Eventually Isabel's selfless love left her life little more than an echo of her father's decay; in short, love meant that if he had to die, she did too.

And so Isabel leaves the world of the young for the world of the sick and the dying. And it is love that takes her there. It is a lopsided love that tilts her totally to her father in need, but away from herself and her own normal needs. To love is to think of the other, never oneself; this is what Isabel believes — but it is killing her. Her love was so selfless that in practicing it she lost any sense of who she was, disappearing totally into the plight of the loved one. Love ought to bring life, but for Isabel it brought inertia and decline. Through love she became nearly as much an invalid as her stroke-stricken father. She is convinced that the cost of pure love is the sacrifice of one's self, and signs of the loss of her self are everywhere: growing indifference to the world outside, even to the point of not knowing what day it was; the lassitude of her spirit and moods; her acceptance of a decay and depression any healthy person would protest. It cannot be denied that Isabel loved her father, but it was a strange and twisted love, not a graced one.

Determining the Essence of Love

What is the nature of love? This is a question with which *Final Payments* struggles, and it is a question any inquiry into the moral life cannot fail to address. There has been a tendency in Christian ethics to elevate selfless love over mutual and reciprocal love; genuine love — the love that most imitates the life and example of Christ — was claimed to be disinterested love, love motivated neither by a desire to be loved nor by a longing for intimacy and fulfillment. Too, the essence of love has often been defined as self-sacrifice, a love heedless of cost and unmindful of reward. In this view, the perfection and excellence of love is determined by what it asks of us; the merit of our love is directly proportionate to its expense. The love that asks everything, feeds on sacrifice, and cares nothing of return is the best love; correspondingly, a love that seeks reciprocity and looks for joy and satisfaction is tainted and ungracious. As Stephen G. Post comments, "Frequently selfless love, a love utterly heedless of self and entirely one-way in its movement, rather than circular, is thought to be ethically superior to communion and alone worthy of the designation 'Christian.'"[6]

A lot of people have been raised to think of love this way, but is such love human? Is it wise to aim for a love "utterly heedless of self"? Our loves should not ignore, much less violate, the deepest needs and inclinations of our nature. Our most fundamental need is not only our need to love, but also our need to be loved in return. One-sided loves are dangerous because they neglect an indispensable part of who we are. The problem in isolating self-sacrifice as the core of Christian love or *agape* is that it promotes an understanding of love that is seriously at odds with who we are. To overcome selfishness we need to be drawn out of ourselves through love, and such love demands sacrifice, exquisite generosity, and sometimes even loss; however, to have a self at all we must be loved, embraced, and cherished in return. The circle of love is what we need, love's give-and-take, love's joyous mutuality, love's ever-deepening union. We need to be generous and extravagant in how we give love, but we equally need to be loved generously and extravagantly in return. It is communion and life we *seek and need* in love, not the self-emptying that makes us disappear.

A viable morality cannot be radically at odds with the deepest needs and inclinations of human beings. It cannot summon us to practice a love that diminishes any more than it can ask us to live without food and drink. If our hearts hunger to be loved passionately and faithfully, this must be celebrated as an ingredient of any healthy love, not an embarrassing and reluctant concession. If we need to be special to someone, singularly cherished by one who wants to bring us to life and in whose love we find peace and our place of belonging, then any account of Christian love must honor this. All love requires expending ourselves, but no love, especially the love of a lifetime, should make us disappear. Love is what makes and keeps us human. If this is so, our expectations of love must be fitted to the facts of who we are. Loves that soar too high can inspire us at a distance but kill us when we make them our own. The love theologians, ethicists, and religious leaders need to prescribe is one that honors who we are in all our dimensions and needs. The best kind of love is not always the most heroic, but the most honestly human. The love that takes into account both our magnanimous possibilities as well as our inescapable limitations is the love we should be taught to esteem.

In recent years a growing number of Christian theologians have acknowledged this. They see the essence of Christian love not primarily as selflessness and sacrifice, but as the mutual care, support, affirmation, and affection through which people build one another up and grow in deeper communion with one another. For them love's principal work is not self-expenditure, but the sharing and generosity through which lovers draw one another more fully to life. In this view the center of love shifts from disinterestedness and sacrifice to reciprocity and communion, and the special power of love is not self-sacrifice, but the mutual gifting of life.[7]

Though love can be costly, at times excruciatingly demanding, the aim of love is not to burden but to draw one more fully to life. Life is what should come of love, not loss and diminishment, not emptiness or despair. Too, the energy of love ought not to be lust for sacrifice, but lust for fuller life, deeper relationships, and richer communion. What ought to be characteristic of any good love is not the sacrifice love often requires, but the gracious power of love to create community and bring life and joy to those who love. As Beverly Wildung Harrison emphasizes,

> Mark the point well: *We are not called to practice the virtue of sacrifice.* We are called to express, embody, share, celebrate the gift of life, and to pass it on! We are called to reach out, to deepen relationship, or to right wrong relations — those that deny, distort, or prevent human dignity from arising — as we recall each other into the power of personhood.[8]

The distinguishing mark of love is not self-sacrifice, but mutually enhanced life. True, there is endless giving involved in love and expansive, often tiresome, generosity; but the purpose of generosity is not sacrifice for its own sake, but building up the other so that he or she can love well in return. The goal of love is not sacrifice, but joyous mutuality leading to true intimacy and communion. And this goal of love suggests something fundamental about ourselves: we are brought to life through the power and creativity of another's love, and that person is brought to life through the power and creativity of our own. There is no other way to be, no other possibility for personhood.

We live because we are loved by somebody — God, to be sure, but many others too. We cannot survive simply by loving, pouring ourselves out day after day. Life requires being loved in return. It is a matter of love meeting love, of each person being drawn more fully to life by the care, goodness, and affection of the other. Each of us *comes to life* in the give-and-take of love, and it is in that dance of love given and love received, of love celebrated and shared, that we *continue in life*. Thus, the core characteristics of love are not selflessness and sacrifice and disinterestedness, but mutual affection, creative benevolence, heartfelt affirmation, and sometimes heartfelt challenge and correction, but all for the sake of friendship, communion, and life. Our love creates others, their love creates us, and the delightful dance of this love is bliss.

What is central to love is the reciprocity of care and affirmation which leads to union. Achieving intimacy and union demands a willingness to give of ourselves generously and faithfully, and it certainly demands conquering a calculating selfishness and egoism, but sacrifice is never an end in itself; rather it is a sometimes necessary means of sustaining the mutual affection and care that are the heart and soul of love, and establishing the communion that is the aim of love.[9] The same was true with Jesus' love. Jesus risked a love that led to his death, but the point of such love was not the sacrifice he was willing to give or the cost he was willing to suffer, but the healing, reconciliation, and communion he desired his death to establish. In short, what was radically innovative in Jesus' love was not its sacrifice, but the alienation it was able to overcome and the absolute community it promised to create, a community so inclusive that he called it the kingdom of God.

Meeting a Woman Unloving and Unlovable

But Isabel Moore has yet to think of love this way. Raised to believe the quintessence of Christian love is sacrifice, it is hard for her to imagine God desiring anything else. Isabel believes those who have passed the test of Christian love are not the ones whose primary loves are with those who love them as well, but the people who are selfless enough to direct their love to the ones they find least lovely. For Isabel, the least lovely of God's creatures is Margaret Casey, a bitter old woman who was her father's former housekeeper. The specter of Margaret hovers over *Final Payments* and haunts Isabel's life. Margaret is the nightmare from which Isabel struggles to awake, the bad dream she keeps reliving. We meet Margaret Casey in this memorable scene:

> At a funeral there is always at least one person one does not wish to see. I looked over at Margaret Casey, who had kept house for us, whom I had not seen in seventeen years. Her coat fit her like a cheese box: an aggressively bad fit. . . . I looked at Margaret, remembering her as she was seventeen years before, when the touch of her damp fingers could sicken me for the afternoon.[10]

Margaret Casey is a woman gone ugly from hatred. Jealousy, anger, pride, and resentment have also disfigured her. She repulses Isabel so completely that the sight of this gnarled, mean woman is enough to make her ill. When Margaret enters a room, all life goes out of it. She is the kind of person whose presence is immediately oppressive, a woman from whom you instinctively withdraw. Margaret Casey is a vicious and vindictive woman, a cruel old shrew adroit at imagining herself slighted so she can envy and begrudge others. Seldom in our lives do we meet people wholly devoid of goodness, but Margaret is one of them. She grows more malicious as she ages, eager to use whatever time is left to her to hurt and malign. This woman who thinks herself a saint has never learned to love anything other than her own jealousy and bitterness. Unloving and unlovable, Margaret exudes hate wherever she goes. No wonder Isabel says "the sound of her slopping around the house in her slippers is the sound of my nightmares."[11]

Nonetheless, even though Isabel was repulsed by Margaret, she was also deathly afraid of becoming like Margaret. She saw in Margaret the tragedy of an ugly and wasted life. There was something about Margaret Casey that represented the absolute perversion of the gift of life; indeed, we see in her what the expression "to fall from grace" means when it is literally embodied. God gives us life to become loving and thoughtful and generous and happy, but Margaret entertained none of those virtues. She had cultivated vicious habits instead: hatred and cruelty, selfishness and maliciousness, bitterness and gloom are what grew in her soul. She had desecrated her life, taking what was meant to be beautiful and graced — something that gave praise and glory to

God—and making it revolting. In place of all the qualities that make us attractive in goodness, Margaret had adorned herself with qualities that leave us morally and spiritually grotesque.

The utter unattractiveness of this woman raises interesting ethical questions: What do we do with people like Margaret Casey? How ought we respond to someone so vile? Most of the time we pray to avoid them, and when forced to deal with them, we do so guardedly, wanting to dispatch of them before harm comes to ourselves. How do we get along with loathsome people? It is not an idle question because eventually we meet them, whether they be in our workplace, in our classes, in our parishes and congregations, or, sadly enough, in our homes.

As we shall see, Isabel responds by trying to love Margaret even though she is the one person Isabel finds nearly impossible to love. It is a clearcut case of trying to love our enemies, and there is certainly no more skilled enemy in Isabel Moore's life than Margaret. But Isabel has no idea how to love Margaret Casey without destroying herself. Her desire to love the enemy she meets in Margaret may be laudable, but the way she practices this love is not, because it nearly kills her. If we answer Jesus' command to love our enemies, we better be astute in doing so. Isabel is not and she pays for her ignorance dearly. We shall see what happens to Isabel when she practices a love doomed from the start, but for now, on the days following her father's funeral, let us walk with her as she reconnects slowly with life.

Reentering Life through the Kindness of Friends

Isabel's all-consuming devotion for her father left her inept at the basic tasks of life. She who had mastered caring for the sick had lost all skill for the normal and the everyday. A woman of thirty, Isabel was overwhelmed at the thought of shopping for clothes, had long ago stopped wearing make-up, and felt defeated by things other women naturally embraced. As she tells her friend Eleanor, "What frightens me is that there are so few things I can *do* anymore. Perfectly normal things that children can do. The smallest thing now makes me feel ruined. Maybe I left it too long."[12]

But Isabel gradually reconnects with the world and she does so through the kindness and love of her friends. Two days after her father's funeral, Eleanor aids Isabel's reentry into the customs and routines of everyday life by promising to take her shopping at Bloomingdale's. In preparation for this journey, Isabel pages through *Vogue* and is stunned to discover how much fashions had changed in the eleven years she had retreated from the world in order to care for her father. But Eleanor helps her. Taking the lead, she assembles a wardrobe for Isabel, picking out things that begin, for Isabel, "this almost Copernican reversal of my way of looking at myself."[13]

Eleanor tailors her kindness to Isabel's need, quietly and astutely preparing her to negotiate a world she could not manage alone. That afternoon shopping expedition to Bloomingdale's was an act of perfect kindness, a beautifully sculpted expression of love, for Eleanor was able to discern and to do exactly what Isabel most needed. It reminds us that doing good is a matter of both substance and style. A truly good person not only sees what needs to be done, but also knows best how to do it. There is an artistry to goodness, and Eleanor exhibits it. She knows how to help Isabel without embarrassing her or making her feel more inept than she already does. Her genius is her capacity to shape the deed so exactly to the situation; in every sense of the word, Eleanor acts fittingly. No clumsy doer of goodness, she demonstrates that virtue is a blend of insight, skill, and precision; it is not just doing good, but doing good in the best and most fitting way possible.

And so with great sensitivity, Eleanor leads Isabel back to life, helping her negotiate all the strangeness of a once familiar world. Through the deftness of her thoughtfulness and the ingenuity of her kindness, Isabel's fears disappear and are replaced by enthusiasm and hope. She gains confidence through Eleanor's love, no longer dismayed by the transition which awaits her, but enthused by the promise of new possibilities. With her friend to steady her, Isabel gets her footing in a world she is suddenly eager to embrace. Realizing she could not manage this transition alone and grateful for the artful kindness of her friend, Isabel reflects,

On the bus to Eleanor's apartment, I looked over at her with a pang of love that was like hunger. How rare Eleanor was, to have kept up with me all those years, to have taken me through this day. I took her hand and squeezed it.

"In many ways," I said, "you've kept me alive."[14]

Isabel recognizes the debts of friendship. During the years her life was swallowed up by the demands of her father, that Isabel survived at all is at least partially attributable to the love and care of friends who refused to abandon her. It reminds us of how often we are steadied and sustained by friends who know us better than we sometimes know ourselves, and who refuse to give up on us when we change in ways they do not understand. Eleanor and Liz, Isabel's closest friends, cared enough for her to remain loyal to Isabel during the eleven years she was largely unmindful of them. At a time when all of Isabel's attention was directed to her father, they were attentive to her, challenging her, sometimes chiding her and growing angry with her, but always steadfastly seeking what was best for her. When Isabel insisted on remaining in the world of the dying, they found ways to renew her in life. The proof of their friendship was their pledge always to believe in something better for her, never giving up on Isabel even when she rejected their love and gave up on herself. It would have been easier, even understandable, for Liz and Eleanor to turn their backs on Isabel, leaving her to shrivel in the world of the dying. But they refused to abandon her, and their patience was a sign not only of remarkable faithfulness, but also of their conviction that this woman they loved deserved something better.

Their friendship was Isabel's lifeline. At a time when she did not care for herself, Liz and Eleanor insisted on caring for her. They exhibited the steadfast availability and generosity that are marks of good friendship, offering themselves to Isabel when she was not able to offer herself to them. Their commitment was not only a sign of their love for her, but also of their unwillingness to allow Isabel to destroy herself. Good friendships are relationships of moral excellence, and the special excellence in Liz and Eleanor's friendship for Isabel was that their devotion to Isabel's good, their concern, care, and unyielding faithfulness, were precisely what brought her life when so much else was killing her.[15] The devotion of Eleanor and Liz reminds us there are times when it is only through the faithful and challenging love of friends that we survive. It also reminds us that there are some debts in life we can never repay.

Meeting a Man Who Lives Only for Himself

But not everyone is capable of friendship. Some people are too selfish to be concerned with the good of another and too calculating to see love as anything more than manipulation. Such a man was Liz's husband John Ryan. After eleven years of no contact with Ryan, Isabel sees him again the day she visits Liz and her children. It is a reunion she does not welcome.

John Ryan is a man who lives only for himself and loves no one other than himself. Everything he does is calculated to further his advantage. Beneath his handsome, friendly appearance is a man so self-absorbed that he approaches everything, including other people, as if he owns it. This is a man moved by nothing but his own interests, a man who sees everyone existing for no other reason than to serve his needs and succor his pleasures. Lurking behind a facade of cheerful sincerity is a man used to having his way and willing to hurt others to get it.

Mary Gordon describes John Ryan as a person of whom to be wary. His character is a warning to all who are lured by his charm into the orbit of his life: here is a selfish, thoughtless man who is careless with the lives of others and indifferent to the pain he brings them. We should not be fooled by his charm or seduced by his banter. This is a man too selfish to do good, a man so driven by his own desires that to come close to him is to be hurt. We should fear such people and we should avoid them. Mary Gordon's point is that such self-centeredness is not benign. The unavoidable consequence of narcissistic self-absorption is violence to the well-being of others, and anyone who has lived with such creatures knows this to be true. We need to beware of people whose guiding principle in life is that everyone and everything exists for their sake, for they will destroy as surely as lovers give life.

Such a man is John Ryan. And yet what baffles and maddens Isabel is that this totally egocentric man is, nevertheless, both quite successful in life and even effective in achieving some good. Here is a man whose whole life had been spent advancing himself regardless of the cost to others; and yet, despite his unwavering self-aggrandizement, not only had he advanced steadily up the ladder of success but was admired as he did so. It does not seem right to Isabel that such calculating selfishness should be rewarded or such blatant hypocrisy succeed.

But if Isabel despises John Ryan, why does she have sex with him? It happens this way. He offers Isabel the job of Director of Project Caretaker. Her job will be to interview elderly persons who live with individuals or families who receive aid from the state to help them care for them. One evening, shortly before the project begins, John Ryan hosts a party for the college students who will be assisting Isabel with the interviews. Isabel attends the party but feels completely out of place. The smiling, eager faces of the students are so foreign to her that she feels isolated and excluded. They are a group to which she could never belong.

This desire to belong — and the insecurity all of us experience when we do not feel included — nudges her to John Ryan. Isabel knows what is happening. John Ryan revolts her, yet she needs to feel included. The discomfort of being a misfit, of finding no one at a party with whom to connect, draws her to a man she knows will only do her harm. Against her better judgment, and knowing whatever she does she will later regret, Isabel approaches John Ryan, thinking, "Most stupid things are done for fear of having no one to talk to."[16] Like all of us, Isabel wants to be liked and wants to belong: "Go on, said something inside me, friendly, poking me in the ribs, laughing but not unkindly. . . . You can't go on like this, it was saying. You don't want to be alone; you don't want to be lonely."[17]

None of us wants to be lonely and all of us want to belong, and sometimes these needs lead us to do things we later sorely regret. Isabel knows John Ryan wants her. She also knows his desire for her has nothing to do with love; she is one more woman for him to conquer and possess. She abhors John Ryan and knows if she lets him seduce her she will be humiliated and ashamed. But her better judgment is overpowered by her desperate need to feel taken by somebody. And so Isabel drives off with John Ryan, knowing that at the end of what is about to happen she will not feel loved but foolish.

Why does Isabel have sex with a man she despises? Why does she do something she knows will only hurt her? Because all of us want to be special to someone and sometimes this need is so strong it pulls us into situations where we know love is counterfeit and affection false. We say yes to things we know will end in hurt and disappointment for the momentary illusion of feeling loved. Isabel's action is stupid and self-destructive, but it is a foolishness we have probably known in ourselves. She was mistaken to give herself to someone as shallow and narcissistic as John Ryan, but she was not misguided in her desire to be cherished by somebody. In order to live we need to be loved, not by evil people like John Ryan whose masquerade at love can only destroy, but by people who delight in us and want to share life with us. Isabel has never known such love, but her fortunes will change when she meets Hugh Slade.

Why We Need to Be Special to Somebody

Isabel sees Hugh for the first time in Liz's kitchen and is immediately attracted to him. There is something about Hugh that Isabel had not found in other men. His gentleness and kindness and quiet self-assurance fascinate Isabel. Within seconds she knows she has met a man she could love, and the mystery of this attraction and its sense of possibilities call her to a boldness she had not experienced before. Not wanting this stranger to slip out of her life, Isabel takes a chance: she invites Hugh to lunch and he accepts.

After Hugh leaves Liz stuns Isabel with the news that he is married, albeit unhappily; however, this does not deter her. Having tasted the possibility of happiness, Isabel will not be dissuaded. Her determination is a measure of her hope, but also of her need. For the first time in her life Isabel senses something promising. Is it temptation or is it grace? Should she embrace this or should she flee in fear? All she knows for sure is that she felt in Hugh the hint of a different kind of love. Love for Hugh will not be like her love for her father, and certainly not like love for Margaret Casey. She knows the hurt, frustration, and disappointment seeking Hugh may bring not only to herself but also to others; and yet, knowing this she cannot turn away. What she has found, she comes to believe, is someone who loves her and wants to make her happy, and she, Isabel thinks, will be happy in loving him. It is this vision of the two of them together, each the beloved of the other, that solidifies Isabel's resolve to pursue Hugh through the thicket of pain and deception which awaits her. She knows she will suffer in loving him and will certainly bring suffering to others; but her desire for any kind of affectionate, passionate, and mutual love, however inaccessible and incomplete, is stronger than the fear of inevitable hurt and loss. What she wants more than anything is to be the beloved of somebody. Watching him walk away after their first lunch together, Isabel says,

> The sight of his back was so beautiful that I felt a kind of despair. If he wanted me, my life would be full of separations. He would always be going away, back to his children, to his wife. It was possible that today I was doing something that would cause pain to strangers, but I did not care. I felt I had finally joined the company of other, ordinary humans. It was the first time I had wanted anything in adulthood: I wanted him. I felt I was capable of extraordinary selfishness. I was saying over and over, "I am the beloved; the beloved is mine."
> And I thought of the depths of selfishness in those words.[18]

What Does It Mean to Love Someone "in God"?

With Hugh, Isabel discovers another kind of love. It is not a love measured by sacrifice and selflessness, but a love overflowing in attractiveness, passion, excitement, pleasure, and joy. She remembers in high school a slogan on the bulletin board: "LOVE IS MEASURED BY SACRIFICE," and being told by Sister Fidelis that she did not have to like someone in order "to love them in God."[19] But even then Isabel protested. What does it mean to love somebody in God? How could that be satisfying for the one being loved?

Isabel's reluctance to heed Sr. Fidelis's advice is based in her conviction that all of us want to be loved, but we want to be loved for who we are uniquely, for our spirit and personality and talents and goodness and gifts — even for our crazy eccentricities — and not because we're mixed in with everyone else in the vast expanse of God's love. And we want to be loved by someone who finds *us* attractive, interesting, and desirable, and not just because a God who loves everybody happens to love us too. To love another person because he or she is in God sounds too ethereal and impersonal to Isabel to be satisfying. It suggests yes we may be loved, but only because each of us is interchangeable with everybody else. To love someone in God, Isabel thinks, is to love them as if they were anybody. But we should, she suspects, love them not as if they were anybody but precisely because they are not. We love them not because we have disregarded their uniqueness, but because we have seen it and prized it. It is because they are who they are, and not someone else, that we love them; it is their specialness (the way they walk, their smile, how they surprise us, what they find funny), not their anonymity, that lures us. The day Sister Fidelis told her she should love another person in God, Isabel remembers thinking,

> But who wants to be loved in God? I had thought then, and still thought. We want to be loved for our singularity, not for what we share with the rest of the human race. We would rather be loved for the color of our hair or the shape of our ankle than because God loves us.[20]

Still, Sr. Fidelis may not have been completely wrong. Isabel is right to challenge any mode of love which blurs our differences and overlooks our uniqueness, but she is wrong to conclude that loving another person in God is to love them in some bland and indiscriminate way. To love someone in God is not to love them less, but to love them in light of their most wondrous individuality because it is to see them in their connection to the God whose goodness draws all things to life and whose creativity makes all things unique. To love a man or woman "in God" is to see him or her most truly and clearly because it is to be drawn to that person's most stunning uniqueness as finely fashioned and absolutely irreplaceable singular images of God. It is to see in the other what God sees, a person of incomparable dignity, a unique child of God whose singular existence testifies that when it comes to loving, no one is more imaginative, more creative, and more delighted by differences than God. Put differently, to love another person in God is to recognize that if we are in love with that person it is only because God was in love with him or her first.

Why Being Loved by God May Not Be Enough for Us

Nonetheless, Isabel was right to insist that everyone hungers to be specially chosen and loved by somebody, and in this sense, knowing we are loved "in God" or even "by God" may not be enough. Not long after she has fallen in love with Hugh Slade, Isabel makes a Christmas visit to her lifelong friend Father Mulcahy. She tells him what she has learned about human beings from her job interviewing the elderly, commenting, "The only thing I can say is that everybody wants to be the most important person in someone's life and most people don't get it." When Fr. Mulcahy responds, "But we're all the most important people in the heart of God," Isabel says, "But you see, that's not enough. . . . I mean people are still lonely; they're still unhappy."[21]

Her point is that love means being specially chosen and singularly preferred over others. Isabel insists that the very nature of love is preferential because exactly what love means is choosing this one person instead of that one, and doing so because we are strongly attracted to her or to him instead of somebody else. She tells Fr. Mulcahy that all of us have a deep need to belong to someone, a need to be linked in love to someone who finds joy and meaning in loving us and in being loved by us. We want and need someone to love us on account of what makes us lovable. We want their love to be a response to, and an affirmation of, our attractiveness and value, an abiding endorsement of our singularity. Isabel cannot accept Fr. Mulcahy's view that being important to God is enough to satisfy us. Yes, we need to know God loves us and we want to think we matter to God; but the best way for God to show we are important is to give us someone who loves us *because* there is nobody else quite like us.

All this comes home to Isabel when she visits Mrs. Riesert, an eighty-seven-year-old woman who is "terribly unhappy" and "cries most of the day."[22] Mrs. Riesert wants to die because she is lonely and has no one who loves her the way she needs to be loved. "What I want is to be with someone who wants me. Wants *me*," she says to

Isabel, "Or else I want to die."[23] Mrs. Riesert had known such love when her husband was alive — the love of absolute preference, of being chosen and cherished above others — but since his death there was "no one left who loved her more than anyone else."[24]

Listening to Mrs. Riesert, Isabel is reminded of herself. In Hugh she has found a man who has singled her out, a man who wants her above others and whom she wants in return. Thanks to Hugh, Isabel has redefined love. She comes to see that the measure of love is not sacrifice and selflessness, but the joy of finding another whose life can be our home — one from whose heart we can live, one who says to us, "It is you I wish to know," and to whom we respond, "It is by you I wish to be known." To give and receive that love, to live in it and to become one through it, is the measure and perfection of love. This is what Isabel has discovered with Hugh and desperately wants to keep.

The Inseparable Connection between Love and Loss

The visit with Mrs. Riesert also teaches Isabel that loves once won can someday be lost. The paradox of love is that we can only know its joy if we make ourselves vulnerable to its pain and possible loss. Love and loss can no more be separated than love and life. If we only come to life through love, it is equally true that life-giving loves can die. And they die in many ways: betrayals, boredom and indifference, everyday negligence and carelessness, infidelities, newly pursued attractions, a growing list of things unforgiven. As with any great good, life-giving loves are ineluctably fragile.

Isabel realizes this in her conversation with Mrs. Riesert. In pursuing love with Hugh Slade she makes herself vulnerable to a terrible potential loss. If she allows herself to be of singular importance to Hugh, and he to herself, she takes a great risk because she gambles the meaning and happiness of her life on the love of a single, irreplaceable person. If there is the potential of great happiness in this kind of love, there is also the potential of great loss. Isabel has found in Hugh, and he in her, someone with whom she identifies her life, her happiness, indeed, her very future. Such love is an incomparable blessing, an unsurpassable gift. But such love is also terribly risky because it demands that we invest ourselves in a blessing that can be taken away.

Mrs. Riesert's loss reminds Isabel of her gamble. "If I let Hugh love me like that, if I said to life, 'This is what I want, only this; I can make do with nothing else,'" she realizes, "then I was immensely vulnerable. It was he I wanted, and even if he wanted me in return, it could not go on forever."[25] The irony of love is that once we find another who seems uniquely suitable for us, we simultaneously recognize love's fragility. Love is fragile, surprisingly given and sometimes just as surprisingly taken away. The risk shadowing every offering and acceptance of love is that if we identify our lives with some irreplaceable good, we make ourselves much more vulnerable to loss. Behind every discovery of love is the sad awareness that love is always imperiled. To locate our happiness, like Isabel, in some singular and irreplaceable good, like loving and being loved by this person and no one else, is to stake the well-being of our lives on a grace that is immensely promising, but also immensely fragile. No wonder love's gratitude always wrestles with fear. Love and loss, they cannot be separated in this world, and it is something Isabel intuits the moment she first realizes Hugh's preciousness *for her.*

> And I said to myself, This is love. It is saying, You are the only one, it could not possibly be any other. It is saying, Without you my life will be immensely impoverished. And I thought of the poverty of my life before this moment of impossible richness, lying in the sun in the middle of December, and I thought of all I would lose when I lost him. There was in me now the new sense of the inevitable and for the first time, of the particular, and in the center of it all, even in the sun, in all this beauty, the first fear of loss, the first foreboding that what I valued was at once irreplaceable and impossible to guarantee. I closed my fingers tightly around his wrist.[26]

Thus, even though the selfless, sacrificial love Isabel had for her father shriveled her, in a way it was much safer, and less challenging, than the embodied, passionate, and singular love she has found with Hugh. The kind of love Isabel has with Hugh is not only more vulnerable to chance and to loss, but also more difficult to practice because it demands openness, because it demands letting ourselves be known by another as completely and truthfully as possible, and because it demands receiving the gift of another into ourself. Loving everyone indiscriminately is relatively easy because it does not demand that we come to know — or be known by — anyone well. It is loving everyone, but at a safe distance, never requiring that we become mixed up in the messy singularities of any person's life, never asking that we remain faithful to that person in a way that we are not and cannot be faithful to others. Selfless, indiscriminate love sounds altruistic, but if it is the only love we practice our loving will be shallow, unchallenging, and altogether too much in our control.

To love we have to get all wrapped up with somebody, including God. That can be messy, frightening, and certainly demanding, but it is also the most human and enriching love, and ultimately the only satisfying love. To love is to risk entangling our life *over time* with another. It is to wager our happiness on investing ourself *faithfully* in the life of a beloved. It is to allow another *to have a claim on us* and to give that person the responsibility of not only caring for us, but also of challenging us. Isabel can avoid this richer but riskier love. She could choose to practice a safer love and thereby avoid the pain of loss and the cost of faithful investment, but if she does she knows she would become like "Margaret who had never taken any risks, who had been content to grow white and small and safe, under the wet blanket of charity, under the dark bell of the familiar."[27] The lesson of *Final Payments* is that we cannot know the gift of love unless we also embrace the risk, the cost, and the possible loss of love.

Why Love Demands Honesty

Isabel experiences dramatically the fragility of love the night she meets Hugh's wife, Cynthia, at a fund-raising party for a liberal Democrat. Cynthia has been told of Isabel's affair by John Ryan, who wants to punish her because she will no longer have sex with him. Ryan points her out to Cynthia, and Cynthia, brimming with anger, bitterness, and hurt, tells Isabel, "You think you're the first, but you're not the first, and you're not even the best looking," adding, "Do you know how many affairs he's been through? Fifteen. Twenty. Do you think I'm going to let you take him from me now?"[28] Wanting to hurt Isabel as Isabel has hurt her, Cynthia says, "You're a very, very sick person.... There is something very wrong with you.... It must be disgusting to be as selfish as you are.... What would your father say if he knew what kind of life you lead?"[29] And in her cruelest blow, she concludes,

> "I know all about girls like you.... You couldn't wait for your father to die so you could get a man between your legs. There's something very wrong with you. There's something disgusting and unhealthy. People like you aren't fit for normal life."[30]

But what stings Isabel the most are not the words Cynthia hopes will hurt, but her almost gentle remark, "You want to be a good person. I know you are a good person at heart. Everything John Ryan has told me about you leads me to believe that you are a good person."[31] Cynthia reminds Isabel of a goodness and innocence she once possessed but now feels she has lost. It is this awareness of virtue lost and integrity tainted that stuns Isabel enough to make her want to recover that goodness no matter how costly doing so might be. She feels that she once had been a good person, a woman beyond reproach, and mourns that lost goodness as a mislaid treasure. She feels pleasure and selfishness led her astray, leaving her hurting people she did not even know and transforming her into a person she never wanted to become. It was her love for Hugh, she concludes, and the delight she found in him, that misled her and opened her to scorn and to shame. Thus, after the encounter with Cynthia, Isabel tells Hugh she does not want to see him again because she wants to be a good person, never hurting anyone. And she wants to retrieve the treasure she had carelessly and thoughtlessly lost. By giving up Hugh, Isabel reasons, she can regain her goodness and innocence and once more live beyond reproach.

Does Being Good Mean Not Being Normal?

And yet Isabel admits that she had gained her pristine goodness at the cost of a normal and healthy life. It was only by sequestering herself in her home with her father and learning to deny certain wants and needs that Isabel gained the reputation of the good daughter and the neighborhood saint. To merit the prize of a virtuous reputation and a life beyond reproach, she had sacrificed much that a normal life demands. Comparing herself to the Virgin Mary, the mother of Christ, she says, "As a reward for the loss of a normal life, she became the mother of God. As the daughter of my father, I thought my fate as inevitable as hers, as forcefully imposed, as impossible to question."[32]

Isabel had become more an icon than a person. The virtue attributed to her by the priests and her pious neighbors had come not so much through Isabel's achievement of actual goodness, but through an abnormal and unhealthy life. She was idealized by everyone as incomparably good (perhaps impossibly good) because she had sacrificed everything that constitutes an ordinary life in order to care for her father. They revered Isabel precisely because her goodness was not ordinary, but never stopped to question whether a life that transgresses some of our most fundamental needs can truly be good. Whatever Isabel gained in the eyes of her worshiping neighbors she lost in the development and health of herself. Too, they honored her for a ghostly, unearthly goodness they never would have demanded of themselves. As Isabel recalled, "I was the good daughter.... Faces were open to me, for mine, they believed, was the face of a saint.... As the daughter of my father I walked in goodness. I was clothed in the white garment of my goodness, visibly a subject of the Kingdom of God."[33]

Isabel gained her goodness by fleeing her creatureliness. She speaks of her life with her father as a kind of sanctuary, a "pure shelter" which guaranteed safety from a threatening and defiling world: "I had brought sanctuary by giving up youth and freedom, sex and life."[34] Hers was not a goodness gained by grappling with life in all its messiness, complexity, and challenges, but by sheltering herself from the situations and relationships out of which genuine goodness grows. Isabel's understanding of goodness demanded relinquishing all the marks of creatureliness: her world, her youth, her body, her freedom, other persons, and her God-given needs.

True virtue is rooted in our creatureliness; it is born from all the passions and attractions of our hearts. True virtue embraces the indisputable givens of our human condition, like love and sex and hunger and freedom, and guides them so that they contribute to our well-being rather than our woe. True virtue works with who we are, which is why the goodness of genuine virtue is tough and earthy and hearty, not sterile and sugary like Isabel's was. There was no wrestling with the challenges and contradictions of life with Isabel, no reckoning with the inescapable needs of her nature. She tried to gain an impossible, and ultimately deceptive, goodness by rejecting the humanity God had given her and meant for her to develop. Most of all, Isabel's goodness was counterfeit because it failed to issue in a healthy, balanced, and genuinely human life. What Isabel failed to realize is that we do not gain goodness by fleeing life and by repressing our nature, but by nurturing and developing all the dimensions of our humanity in the wisest and most promising ways.

A Curious Strategy for Renewal

Isabel first tries to retrieve the goodness and innocence she feels she lost in loving Hugh by cutting her ties with everyone and everything she believes changed her into a woman she was never meant to be. If loving Hugh had made her selfish and indifferent to the hurt she caused others, she would begin her rehabilitation by abandoning Hugh. When he pleads with her to reconsider, Isabel speaks to him not as a man she once loved, but as to a child with whom she must be stern. And when she sends him away, vowing never to see him again, Isabel announces that she, shriven and repentant, will begin her new life by going to live with the woman she has always most despised, Margaret Casey. Angry and bewildered, Hugh slaps Isabel, screaming, "Your father's dead, you're not dead. You have a life. Why do you want to take your life?"[35]

Isabel is too dazed to be stirred by the truth in Hugh's remark. He is right that by going to live with Margaret, Isabel will destroy the life she is meant to savor. She thinks that by becoming indifferent to all she once desired and loved, particularly Hugh, she can become good again. She thinks she will cleanse her soul by turning her back on what is most dear to her, because if she wants nothing and is attached to nothing she will not hurt anyone ever again. She believes absolute detachment will make her whole.

But she is wrong. Even before she moves in with Margaret, we see what Isabel's backwards strategy for virtue will do to her. She immediately slides into the deterioration and gloom that marked her life with her father. To retrieve her precious goodness she withdraws from life, hiding in her bedroom where she eats and sleeps, sleeps and eats, never seeing anyone, never doing anything, as she grows pale, fat, and listless. She quits her job, refuses to talk to her friends, and spends her days in bed, certain that solitude and seclusion will keep her good and insure that she sins no more.

And so Isabel once more becomes an invalid. If all-absorbing care for her father crippled her before, trying to protect some imaginary goodness by cutting all ties with life shrivels her now. Isabel thinks the only way she can avoid harming others is by keeping company only with herself and the woman she finds nearly impossible to love. But the price of her delusion is not only a terribly desolate life, but one untouched by hope. In her misguided strategy to recover innocence, Isabel walks away from a world marked by friendship and love, grace and promise, beauty and joy, to withdraw into the safe but hopeless world of the psychologically and emotionally comatose. Seeking a life of absolute apathy and detachment, she retreats into her room to find virtue in her sleep and sainthood in her dreams.

There is something sad and pathetic and foolish in Isabel's total withdrawal from life, but there is also something extraordinarily selfish. Ironically, Isabel chastises herself for having grown selfish in her love and desire for Hugh and the pleasures she found there; however, what she does not see is that there is also something terribly self-absorbed in her obsessive preoccupation with her own goodness and perfection. There is nothing more selfish than striving for a goodness that can be had only by neglecting the people we love and who love us, nothing more narcissistic than being so concerned with our own virtue that we cannot risk being concerned about others. Isabel is deceived because she who reproached herself for having made herself the "center of the universe" with Hugh, does not realize that in her absolute and eerie seclusion she is once more the center of her world, although a very small and lonely world it is.

An Attempt at an Illusory Love

And so Isabel leaves the love of preference and pleasure and desire she had with Hugh, for the love of indifference and sacrifice and selflessness with Margaret. "I had loved Hugh, had said . . . only this person and no other," Isabel reflects. "But I would not live like that again. I would love whoever most needed loving, and then go on, for there would always be someone else, anyone else, if it was not pleasure you cared for."[36]

Her error, she thinks, was loving the one who loved and needed her, and whom she loved in return. Her dreadful mistake was pursuing a love she found attractive and pleasurable, embracing a man she preferred instead of attaching herself to whatever stranger crossed her path. She loved Hugh because he was lovable, and because she found loving him life-giving and uplifting, but that, Isabel now thinks, was wrong. She had been painfully fooled in pursuing a love that told her she was prized by another. Her error, Isabel is sure, was thinking love was meant to be personal and rich, centered on the man who could delight in her as she could in him.

She was wrong to look for joy and life in love, wrong to love for pleasure. She would now love not for pleasure but for sacrifice. She would repent of her wayward love with Hugh by handing herself over to the woman she loved not at all, the woman who knew best how to make herself Isabel's enemy, the spiteful Margaret Casey, beloved perhaps to God, but abhorrent to everyone else. It is by changing her object of devotion, from Hugh who loves her to Margaret who wants to destroy her, that Isabel thinks she will once more be good. "I would take care of Margaret; I would devote myself to the person I was least capable of loving," she resolves. "I would absorb myself in the suffering of someone I found unattractive."[37] But she also thinks that in loving Margaret she will best imitate the love of God:

> I would love Margaret now as God loved His creatures: impartially, impervious to their individual natures and thus incapable of being really hurt by them. . . . I could not love with God's intensity. But I would choose His mode: the impartial, the invulnerable, removed from loss.[38]

The Love of God Revisited

Isabel is right to want to imitate the love of God, but does she rightly understand how God loves? She describes a God who loves everybody equally but impersonally. The love of God, she thinks, is spontaneous and unmotivated, prompted not by anything in us that might be worthy of love, but simply because it is the nature of God to love. Isabel envisions a divine love that is so absolutely impartial that it appears indifferent to our individuality. Such a love may be universal and unconditional, but it is also oddly unconnected to any quality in ourselves that might make us lovable. God loves us unfailingly, Isabel thinks, but with no regard to who we actually are; in short, Isabel describes a God who loves us without ever having to know us. For her there is no link between why God loves us and who we are. The divine love is universal and unconditional, but it is also distant and impersonal, a blind, random love that never ventures close enough to see who we really are.

Too, Isabel describes a divine love that seeks nothing and wants nothing. There is no notion here of God wanting to be loved in return, no indication that a God who loves all might long to be loved too, and certainly no sign that there might be anything attractive in us that God might find lovable. Isabel never thinks of God being disappointed at our failures to love or hurt by our unfaithfulness. She never speaks of God seeking friendship with us or of being gratified by our offerings of love. Rather, she imagines a God whose love is so detached and indifferent that it matters little whether we love God or not. Too, the God Isabel describes as the perfect lover remains strangely untouched and unmoved by the very ones he loves. Such a God could never weep when we weep or rejoice with us when we are happy. Isabel's God is forever safe from loss (or from gain) because her God is not really invested and involved in us. Isabel's perfect lover — her supreme being — is oddly cold and remote by refusing to feel, to be moved, or to suffer. It is hard to imagine why being loved by Isabel's God would matter to us, how we could ever worship such a God, or why we would think such a God's love was love at all.

But God's love may be quite different than Isabel thinks. Although it is true theologians have sometimes affirmed the understanding of divine love Isabel proposes, more recently many have suggested that

God both desires and actively seeks a relationship of love with us because God, who created us in the divine image, finds us lovable and very much wants to be loved by us in return. God's love, they suggest, is passionate, motivated, and interested; indeed, it can even be described as erotic inasmuch as God seeks to be "all wrapped up" in our lives and hopes we will be "all wrapped up" in the divine life. If we think of love as a "will to belong," perhaps God wills to belong to us as much as, and probably more than, we desire to belong to God.[39] After all, God has consistently demonstrated the heartfelt desire to belong to us and to be "all wrapped up" in our lives through the offer of grace, through the gift of Jesus, through the continuous presence of the Spirit, and through the sacraments, particularly the eucharist. Each of these testifies to God's intense desire to be intimate to our lives.

Contrary to what Isabel thinks, to say that God loves everybody is not to claim that God's love is abstract and impersonal, but that God is infinitely capable of prizing our uniqueness and savoring our particularity *because that is what love is* and God is the perfection of love. There are no defects of love in God. We would hardly claim that anyone who loved us as if we were anybody loved us well, and we should never think of God, who is the essence and perfection of love — indeed, the very revelation of love — loving like that either. Quite the contrary, God can love us better than anyone exactly because God knows us better than anyone, seeing us with more insight and ingenuity than anyone else. And like any true lover, God wants to be loved in return. What God seeks with us is a community of love, a fellowship in which love given is love received, celebrated, and returned. What Isabel fails to realize is that the essence of love, even for God, is not self-sacrifice and selflessness, but mutuality and communion.

But Isabel is mixed-up about how God loves. And so she goes to live with Margaret because she presumes what God wants is for us to love the person least likely to love us in return. Arriving at Margaret's dreary home, Isabel thinks, "The greatest love is to love without wanting anything in return, even an acknowledgment of loving. And this is how I would love."[40] Isabel makes herself utterly pliable to Margaret's malice and cruelty; she acts as if the surest proof of Christian love is to allow oneself to be victimized by another's rampant loveless-ness. And so she lets herself be battered by that ugly woman's hatred and viciousness. Day after day Margaret humiliates and ridicules Isabel, missing no opportunity to demean her. She lives to work revenge on every slight she imagines she has suffered, especially from Isabel on whom she blames all the sadness and emptiness of her life. Margaret's meanness devastates Isabel, each little cruelty another blow to her spirit; but she receives these taunts meekly, convinced there is no greater proof of love than to allow one's destruction at the hands of an enemy. "Margaret had defeated me, but I would go on loving her," Isabel explains to herself. "Because Margaret was the person I found most difficult to love."[41]

Why Love Is Gratitude for a Gift

Isabel's choice to surrender all her love to a woman who delights in hating her almost kills her. But two things happen which begin Isabel's movement back to life. First, she receives a letter from Hugh, which says simply, "My dearest: I ache for you. I long for you. I am always waiting for you. Hugh."[42] This note rekindles desire in her. With these few words from Hugh, the spell of Isabel's sick love is broken as her obsession with selflessness and sacrifice is replaced by passionate desire and rekindled longing.

Isabel reconnects with life through the power of desire. She begins to find the strength necessary to leave behind a sick love when she is no longer embarrassed to acknowledge an erotic and embodied love. Indeed, her resurrection begins when she rediscovers wants and longings, attractions and desires. She will recover through a love resplendent with hunger and desire because to be human *is to hunger and desire*. Isabel had tried to live without desiring, but for human beings such absolute apathy is death. To live is to long for something to fill our hearts and to bless our spirits, it is to hunger for something to embrace. Desiring, wanting, longing, loving, these are the passions by which we live and grow.

The second thing that contributes to Isabel's gradual return to life is a visit she receives from her old friend Fr. Mulcahy. He tells Isabel she should leave Margaret and come home. When Isabel says she cannot because she had made a promise to love Margaret no matter what, Fr. Mulcahy responds, "Even God breaks promises."[43] And when the priest leaves to return to the city, he tells Isabel to watch her weight and take care of her beauty, saying, "God gave you beauty. If you waste it, that's a sin against the fifth commandment." She asks, "Thou shalt not kill? What does that have to do with it?" and Fr. Mulcahy responds, "It means slow deaths, too."[44]

The priest reminds Isabel that in practicing a pointless and impossible love she is sinning against herself, against all those who truly love her, and against a God who loves her too and wants her to find a love that will make her happy. To love rightly we must learn the nature, needs, and limits of love, and Isabel clearly has not. Fr. Mulcahy's point is that no love should ever lead to the annihilation of ourself. By persisting in a love that does nothing more than make Isabel victim to a woman who is happy to destroy her, Isabel, as Fr. Mulcahy observes, becomes an accomplice to her own death, and that is a sin. That kind of love is a violation of everything God wants for us; indeed, it violates the reason God gives us life. The priest reminds Isabel that God gifts us with life so that we can love and be loved. That is not possible for Isabel if she stays with Margaret Casey; indeed, for Isabel to remain there is for her to transgress what God, and everyone who loves her, wants for her.

How Are Our Enemies to Be Loved?

Can Isabel love an enemy such as Margaret? Christians say we can and we should; in fact, Jesus says it is what distinguishes the love his disciples are called to practice from the everyday love of the pagans. But we should think about this. Does it make sense to love people who are determined to do us harm? Does it make sense to love people who are happy when we fail and who rejoice at our defeats? It certainly doesn't make sense to love them as Isabel loves Margaret Casey. Margaret is her enemy, and for Isabel to make her the singular love of her life is not only foolish and sick, but also a failure on Isabel's part to properly love herself. Jesus tells us to love our neighbors *as ourselves,* and in making herself a victim to Margaret Casey's maliciousness, Isabel violates Jesus' gospel command for a healthy and proper love of self. Jesus tells us to love our enemies, not necessarily to live with them, and certainly not to let them destroy us. He counsels us to avoid hatred for them in our hearts and to refuse to show to them the animosity they extend to us, lest their hatred become our own. But nowhere does Jesus say in order to love the Margaret Caseys of our world we have to stop loving everyone else, including ourselves.

And so how should Isabel love Margaret Casey? She can pray for her, wish her well, hope she repents, stops hating, and grows in the love from which God made her; but she cannot make Margaret the singular love of her life. She can pray that Margaret changes, that she is healed of the resentment and envy and bitterness that have poisoned her heart and guaranteed her unhappiness, and she should grieve that Margaret persists in attitudes and actions that harm her relationships not only with other people, but also with the God she claims to know and to love; but Isabel should not invest the whole of her life in someone who lives only to destroy her as much as she is surely destroying herself.

It is foolhardy for Isabel to waste all the love she can give on a wretched woman who hates her when so many others are eager to love her and be loved by her in return. Isabel can love Margaret, but she better do so from afar because Margaret will not love her. The mortal danger of practicing a completely selfless love on a woman like Margaret is that it not only is unlikely to change the heart of one already hardened and dead, but it also robs the selfless lover of life as well. Everyone dies in this masquerade of love, Isabel who believes she is doing good, and Margaret who is too spiteful to love anyone at all.

Being Extravagant with Our Affection

All of this comes home to Isabel when she recalls the gospel story of Jesus visiting Lazarus, Martha, and Mary at their home in Bethany. When Jesus sits down at table, Mary breaks open "a pound of costly perfume made from genuine aromatic nard" (John 12:3) and with it anoints Jesus' feet. Judas Iscariot objects that the perfume should not be used so extravagantly, but should instead be sold and the money given to the poor. To this Jesus replies, "Leave her alone. . . . The poor you always have with you, but me you will not always have" (Jn 12:7–8).

For the first time Isabel understands the meaning of the story. Jesus was not being indifferent to the plight of the poor, but was suggesting that we should never deprive our loved ones of the gift of our love and the extravagance of our affections. There will never be a shortage of Margarets in the world — hateful, loveless people whose malice gobbles up life — but we are not to squander the riches of our love on them; rather we are to expend our love generously and passionately and abundantly on the ones who can truly receive our love as the life-giving gift it is meant to be, and who are eager and happy to love us in return. "What Christ was saying, what he meant," Isabel realizes, "was that the pleasures of that hair, that ointment, must be taken. . . . We must not deprive ourselves, our loved ones, of the luxury of our extravagant affections. We must not try to second-guess death by refusing to love the ones we loved in favor of the anonymous poor."[45] Isabel sees that she had been a Judas with her love. Instead of investing her love in those to whom she felt attraction and affection, she poured her love into the twisted soul of Margaret Casey, a woman who could never appreciate the gift she had been given.

Isabel's mistake was to think that any love based in preference, inclination, and attraction fell short. Her terrible error was to think loving those she really wanted to love was somehow to fail in love, as if the only love that was not defective, and therefore godly, was selfless, sacrificial love. What she did not realize is that even though we are called to love all of our neighbors, we are not called to love them all in the same way. It is only natural that we love some more than others; in fact, justice demands that we do. Husbands should love their wives more than women they know at work, and parents should love their own children more than they love the children of a friend. Christian love demands that we want the best for everybody, but it does not demand that we love everybody equally; contrary to what Isabel thought, that is not the perfection of love but a failure in love. Christian love demands that we want the greatest possible good for all people, namely, everlasting happiness and friendship with God, but it does not ask that we have the same intensity of affection or depth of love for everyone, nor that we love everyone in the same way.

Finding Our Place of Belonging

Love is a kind of gravitational pull that we experience more strongly with some than others. It is through the attraction and pull of concrete, particular loves that we find our place of belonging in life. That we are drawn to love some persons more intensely and completely than others is not a shortcoming of our nature, but a good indication of who it is best for us to love. Genuine Christian love does not work against the basic inclinations of our nature and the most enduring attractions of our hearts, but orders and fulfills them. In other words, Isabel should love Margaret Casey, but neither as much as, nor to the same degree as, she loves her friends Eleanor, Liz, Fr. Mulcahy, and Hugh.

What Isabel sees now is that the love God most wants us to practice is not the selfless, sacrificial love she struggled to give Margaret, but the rich and extravagant love Mary practiced on Christ when she broke open the jar of perfume and anointed his feet. This insight frees her to accept that her place of belonging — her true home — is not with Margaret Casey, but with her friends: "I knew now I must open the jar of ointment. I must open my life. I knew now that I must leave."[46] Isabel resolves to make no more payments to selfless love, but to invest her heart in loves that can bless her with life. And so she calls Eleanor to take her home, fearing that if she stays a moment longer with Margaret she will die.

At the end of *Final Payments*, Isabel has learned, and finally accepted, the nature and limits of human love. Recognizing that with Margaret she had paid too great a price for love and realizing, thanks to her friends, the love men and women can and should give, Isabel, who for years had been paralyzed by false and dangerous ideas about love, was finally free to live. She accepts now what should never be denied: love is meant to be a path to life, not diminishment, and we are to invest the balance of our loves in those able and eager to love us in return. And so on what happens to be Easter weekend, Isabel leaves a place of death in order to return to life.

In the middle of the night Eleanor arrives to rescue Isabel, and Liz is with her. Seeing the women who had never turned away from her when she insisted on dying, Isabel thinks, "For they had come the moment I called them, and they were here beside me in the fragile and exhilarating chill of the first dawn."[47] The three friends drive away, leaving Margaret Casey in her gloom. And at thirty years of age, Isabel, a woman who for so long had been stricken by a love that soared too high, was finally ready to live.

In conversation with Mary Gordon's *Final Payments* we have probed the nature and limits of love. We explored the nature of God's love, noting similarities between how God loves and how we are called to love, but we also stressed that God can love in ways we cannot. We discovered that the essence of authentic love consists not in sacrifice and self-denial, but in the mutuality, generosity, affirmation, affection, and delight by which love brings life. We reflected on how love differs according to the various relationships of our lives, insisting that even though God calls us to love everyone, love for a spouse, a parent, a daughter, or a friend should be very different from love for an enemy. Many other authors have investigated aspects of these themes. The following works may be helpful for anyone who wishes to reflect further on the nature and importance of love, as well as the cost in never learning how to love.

Dubus, Andre, "A Father's Story"
———, *Voices from the Moon*
Eliot, George, *Middlemarch*
———, *The Mill on the Floss*
Hamill, Pete, *Snow in August*
Hassler, Jon, *Staggerford*
Hillesum, Etty, *An Interrupted Life*
Huth, Angela, *Invitation to the Married Life*
Kingsolver, Barbara, *The Bean Trees*
Sparks, Muriel, *Memento Mori*
Tyler, Anne *Breathing Lessons*
———, *Ladder of Years*
Walker, Alice, *The Color Purple*

Notes

1. The phrase "the limits of love" was suggested to me by Gilbert Meilaender's book *The Limits of Love: Some Theological Explorations* (University Park: Pennsylvania State University Press, 1987), especially chapter 1, "Goodbye, Sally, Goodbye," 15–18.

2. Mary Gordon, *Final Payments* (New York: Ballantine Books, 1979). Subsequent page references to the novel refer to this a edition only. Different editions, of course, will have different page references.

3. Gordon, 14. **4.** Gordon, 5. **5.** Gordon, 6.

6. Stephen G. Post, *A Theory of Agape: On the Meaning of Christian Love* (Cranbury, N.J.: Associated University Presses, 1990), 17. A classical treatment of this understanding of Christian love can be found in Søren Kierkegaard's *Works of Love* (New York: Harper & Row, 1962), and Anders Nygren's *Agape and Eros,* trans. Philip S. Watson (New York: Harper & Row, 1969).

7. Examples of this view include Beverly Wildung Harrison, "The Power of Anger in the Work of Love: Christian Ethics for Women and Other Strangers," in *Making the Connections: Essays in Feminist Social Ethics,* ed. Carol S. Robb (Boston: Beacon Press, 1985), 3–21; Post, *A Theory of Agape;* Edward Collins Vacek, *Love, Human and Divine: The Heart of Christian Ethics* (Washington, D.C.: Georgetown University Press, 1994); Stephen J. Pope, *The Evolution of Altruism and the Ordering of Love* (Washington, D.C.: Georgetown University Press, 1994).

8. Harrison, "The Power of Anger in the Work of Love," 19–20.

9. For an excellent treatment of this point see Christine E. Gudorf, "Parenting, Mutual Love, and Sacrifice," in *Women's Consciousness, Women's Conscience,* ed. Barbara Hilkert Andolsen, Christine E. Gudorf, and Mary D. Pellauer (San Francisco: Harper & Row, 1985), 175–91.

10. Gordon, 6–7. **11.** Gordon, 27. **12.** Gordon, 49. **13.** Gordon, 48. **14.** Gordon, 51.

15. For an analysis of the moral excellence of friendship, see Paul J. Wadell, *Friendship and the Moral Life* (Notre Dame, Ind.: University of Notre Dame Press, 1989), and Lawrence A. Blum, *Friendship, Altruism, and Morality* (London: Routledge & Kegan Paul, 1980), especially pp. 67–83.

16. Gordon, 139. **17.** Gordon, 139. **18.** Gordon, 168. **19.** Gordon, 175. **20.** Gordon, 175. **21.** Gordon, 219. **22.** Gordon, 228. **23.** Gordon, 229. **24.** Gordon, 230. **25.** Gordon, 231. **26.** Gordon, 197. **27.** Gordon, 232. **28.** Gordon, 236. **29.** Gordon, 240. **30.** Gordon, 240–41. **31.** Gordon, 241. **32.** Gordon, 237–38. **33.** Gordon, 238. **34.** Gordon, 239. **35.** Gordon, 245. **36.** Gordon, 248. **37.** Gordon, 249. **38.** Gordon, 260–61.

39. Post, *A Theory of Agape,* 24.

40. Gordon, 264. **41.** Gordon, 267. **42.** Gordon, 284. **43.** Gordon, 297. **44.** Gordon, 297. **45.** Gordon, 298. **46.** Gordon, 299. **47.** Gordon, 307.

CHAPTER FOUR

JUSTICE

Learning to Live with Others in Mind

N EAR THE END of Athol Fugard's *My Children! My Africa!*, a play
exploring life in South Africa under apartheid, Anela Myalatya,
a high school teacher known as Mr. M, speaks to Thami Mbikwana,
his bright but disillusioned student. Mr. M, who strove to instill visions
of hope in students who each day saw more reasons for despair, tells
Thami he recently witnessed something that mocked "all my visions
of splendor."[1] One evening while watching television, Mr. M saw an
Ethiopian tribesman "carrying the body of a little child that had died
of hunger in the famine . . . a small bundle carelessly wrapped in a few
rags." As he looked closely at this image of numb suffering and grief,
Mr. M tells Thami, "I couldn't tell how old the man was. The lines
of despair and starvation on his face made him look as old as Africa
itself."[2] The man brought the child to a massive common grave, but
when he reached the open pit "he didn't have the strength to kneel and
lay it down gently. . . . He just opened his arms and let it fall."[3]

This image of the Ethiopian tribesman, exhausted and without
hope, letting the tiny child slip from his arms into a grave where it
will keep company with all those whose deaths were as anonymous as
their lives, scorches Mr. M's consciousness. It becomes for him not
only a picture of a single tragic death, but a metaphor for all of Africa.
For all around him Mr. M sees the macabre mastery of injustice as a
continent's people are crushed each day by the world's selfishness and
indifference. The grim and eerie picture of the Ethiopian tribesman
walking across the desert plains about to make another offering to the
awful tyranny of injustice, symbolizes what Mr. M sees happening

every day to lives that are wasted and destroyed with little protest from the prosperous. "They are more than just themselves," Mr. M explains. "The tribesmen and dead child do duty for all of us, Thami. Every African soul is either carrying that bundle or in it."[4] The Ethiopian tribesman and the little child carry the scars of injustice and are a vivid, disturbing reminder that injustice is an abstraction only for those who practice it. For those who suffer it, however, injustice is as real as the life they are losing. At one end of the spectrum of injustice are those who prosper by selfishness and indolence and greed, and who soothe what little conscience they have by denial and indifference. But Mr. M recognizes in the Ethiopian tribesman and the corpse of the little child the fate of those who live at the other end of that spectrum, and he sees there a people burdened and denied, and each day encouraged to die. What Mr. M perceives in the death of that nameless child is not an exception to how the world works, but indeed the innermost secret to how the world works. After all, in order for a few to have everything they want as soon as they want it, somebody has to be invited to die long before they ever had a chance to live.

Indifference to the fate of those judged not to matter is the scandal of injustice and the core of its evil. What confounds Mr. M is that so many in other parts of the world can live undisturbed while their brothers and sisters are dying. He tells Thami, "What is wrong with this world that it wants to waste you all like that ... my children ... my Africa! My beautiful and proud young Africa!"[5] Mr. M knows the problem is not with Africa, but with a world in which some who prosper are content to let millions suffer and die. There is something deeply wrong, indeed sinful, with a world in which some grab more than they could possibly need while others are given nothing at all. There is something terribly wrong with a world in which the denial of life for millions is seen to be the inevitable, and even acceptable, cost of waste and excess for a few. Mr. M grasps the scandal of injustice, the intolerable immorality of wasting the lives of millions so that the wealthy can find new ways to be amused.

The fundamental rule of justice is that we harm no one and fulfill our obligations to all. But for this to happen, Johann Baptist Metz observes, the wealthy and prosperous must "learn to 'live differently' so that others should be able to live at all."[6] Both of these points are woven throughout Athol Fugard's *My Children! My Africa!*, a play which movingly, and often disturbingly, examines the absolute lack of justice for the vast majority of South Africans whose lives were twisted and crushed by apartheid, a socially enforced policy of oppression and exclusion that was intentionally designed to insure well-being for a powerful minority, but a wholly diminished life for anyone whose skin happened not to be white.

But it would be a mistake to read this play as if its message mattered only for South Africans. Its focus is there, but its meaning is universal because the obligations of justice are ignored worldwide. If *My Children! My Africa!* looks specifically at the special tragedy of apartheid's injustice, it does so only to prod us to think of how patterns of privilege in power and wealth bring advantages and prosperity for some, but desolation and hopelessness for others. Do we live in a way that insures another anonymous child will be dropped into an unmarked grave somewhere in the world? Do our patterns of consumption guarantee that for some of our sisters and brothers life will never be anything more than a constant struggle to survive? The message of this play is not only that apartheid had to end if South Africa was to survive, but also that injustice everywhere must be confronted if the scandal of stunted lives and stillborn hopes is to be overcome. In too many places of the world too many people are robbed of life because others find it advantageous to live unjustly. The call to a conversion to justice is an absolute obligation, not a lifestyle option, because injustice kills wherever it flourishes. It kills somebody every second of every day. It is dancing on the grave of somebody's lost life now, and to allow that to happen is as ugly an evil as we can imagine.

My Children! My Africa! is a call for conversion and transformation in ourselves and in the patterns and practices of our world so that all who are now denied life can receive what they deserve. We shall explore this and other themes developed in the play by focusing on three points: (1) what justice is and what it seeks to achieve; (2) what injustice denies; and (3) how injustice is overcome and justice restored.

What Justice Is and What It Seeks

My Children! My Africa! opens with a debate between Thami Mbikwana of Zolile High, located in a black township, and Isabel Dyson
of Camdeboo Girls High, a school in a wealthy white area of the
city. Mr. M is moderator for the debate and the proposition to be discussed that afternoon is: "That in view of the essential physical and
psychological differences between men and women, there should be
correspondingly different educational syllabuses for the two sexes."[7]
Thami argues in favor of traditional African culture. He holds that
because of important differences between men and women, especially
physical differences, women cannot do the same jobs as men and must
have different roles in the family and society. He concludes his speech
by saying, "These facts taken together reinforce what our fathers, and
our grandfathers and our great-grandfathers knew; namely that happiness and prosperity for the tribe and the nation is achieved when
education of the little ladies takes these facts into consideration."[8]

Isabel, of course, argues the opposite. She admits her respect for
many of the values of traditional African society, but warns Thami's
fellow students, the audience for the debate, not to be fooled by those
who appeal to long-established customs to block social change or who
equate differences with inferiority, not distinctive strengths. But it is
the ominous note in her closing remarks that turns the debate in Isabel's
favor and convinces Thami's classmates to support her:

> And lastly, a word of warning. The argument against equality for
> women, in education or any other field, based on alleged "differ-
> ences" between the two sexes, is an argument that can very easily
> be used against any other "different" group. It is an argument
> based on prejudice, not fact.[9]

Isabel's point is that if differences between men and women are seen
not as complementary strengths but as assets in men and weaknesses
in women, and thus used to justify discrimination against women, this
same argument can be used against anyone whose "difference" leaves

them outside the dominant power group. The link between their debate topic and the social policy of apartheid could not be more obvious. Isabel warns Thami's classmates about any system in which differences mean superiority and advantages for some but inferiority and exclusion for others, which is exactly what apartheid institutionalized. The whole rationale of apartheid, as well as any systemic injustice, whether it be in society, the churches, or our political and economic structures, is to justify permanent inferiority and exclusion for persons or groups precisely on account of what makes them different, whether it be color, gender, race, religion, social and political beliefs, or sexual orientation.

Ironically, in this classroom debate Thami, in his defense of traditional African customs, articulates the arguments white Afrikaners used against black South Africans to sustain apartheid. When he argued that education and employment opportunities must be fitted to match women's lesser abilities, he expressed exactly the logic of apartheid that undergirded the separate and inferior Bantu education for blacks. In reality, Bantu education was intentionally designed to foreclose equal possibilities for learning, employment, and advancement for black South Africans in comparison with white South Africans, and this deliberate discrimination was justified by the falsehood that black South Africans by nature were inferior in intelligence and ability. Thus, to expect them to perform on an equal level with white South Africans was actually to be unfair to them because it was not to take their limited capacities into account.

The same argument Thami offered in defense of traditional roles for African women was seized by the Afrikaner as the crucial principle in the elaborate justification for apartheid, an overarching policy of discrimination and control which organized society on the basis of supposed superiority for whites and presumed inferiority for blacks, and reinforced that belief through social, economic, and political practices. Apartheid was the social policy which saw what was different in black South Africans, namely, their color, as proof of their inferiority, and took this presumed inferiority into account at every level of society. But what was officially espoused as a prudent concession to differences was actually a cynical rationale for perpetual subjugation. Thus, when Thami allowed "differences" between men and women to legitimate inequity, he did not grasp how the same argument had been used by white South Africans to enshrine social policies whose singlemost purpose was to restrict and dominate black South Africans.

But this is true with any policy, practice, system, or structure that is inherently unjust. When differences are read to mean inferiority and exclusion, injustice is ready to flower because people no longer see each other as sisters and brothers who complement one another in their differences, but as persons and nonpersons in a world where it is perfectly fitting for some to dominate and exploit and for others to be oppressed and denied. Inevitably, what results are social, political, economic, educational, and even ecclesiastical structures and practices carefully designed to limit the power and opportunities of those deemed not only inferior, but often even less than human.

At the conclusion of the debate, Mr. M asks Thami's classmates to vote for whose argument they found most persuasive, Thami's or Isabel's. To his surprise and joy, Isabel is declared the winner. He tells her, "It wasn't easy for that audience to vote against Mbikwana. He's one of them, and a very popular 'one of them' I might add."[10] As much as Mr. M is proud of his star pupil, he is glad Thami's views did not prevail. By listening carefully to Isabel and allowing themselves to be influenced by her arguments, Thami's classmates were able to break through to a new and more insightful understanding of their African traditions. While acknowledging the values in much of the tradition, they also came to see how it could be an unsuspected source of injustice. Isabel won the debate because she helped the students recognize the subtle strategies of injustice. Unjust policies and practices always hide behind arguments which are meant to sound reasonable, logical, even benevolent and compassionate. They are enshrined in traditions which are venerated as wise and unquestionable, and thus never open to change, but their aim is always to exalt some and degrade others.

The debate was a moment of enlightenment in which the students were able to break free from their own certainties and biases in order to recognize how some things we take for granted can be terribly wrong. In fact, what was most impressive about the debate were not the arguments so passionately delivered by Thami and Isabel, but that the students were open to another point of view. By listening to Isabel and by not being ruled by bias and fear, they were able (and willing) to be challenged and changed. This is no small accomplishment. The afternoon debate at Zolile High School demonstrated that the movement from injustice to justice is possible only when people are able and willing to move beyond their customary perspectives and opinions, and to be open to other points of view. In short, justice requires people of openness, humility, and receptivity, people who allow themselves to be touched and influenced by those who are "different," those whose experience of the world, precisely because of those differences, is not their own.

The great accomplishment of Thami's classmates is that they did not allow tradition or prejudice or fear to block enlightenment — they listened to Isabel with open hearts and open minds. And Mr. M rejoices at Isabel's victory because he knows the changes necessary for justice and peace can come only if people are willing to do exactly what Thami's classmates did: to listen to what they would normally dismiss and to receive the very ones they would almost always reject. That they were able to look upon Isabel not as an outsider or an enemy, but to welcome her, listen to her, and be changed by her is what gives Mr. M hope. As he says to Thami, "But the fact that you didn't succeed is what makes me really happy. I am very proud of our audience. In my humble opinion they are the real winners this afternoon. You two just had to talk and argue. Anybody can do that. They had to listen...intelligently!"[11]

The Virtue That Governs Our Relations with Others

Isabel won the debate by appealing to the students' instinctive sense of justice and their deeper awareness that anything which violates justice is terribly wrong. But what exactly is justice? One of the four "cardinal" or principal virtues essential for life (the other three being prudence, temperance, and fortitude), justice governs our relations with others by insuring that we respect their dignity as human beings and give them their due. It is the virtue of human togetherness that calls our attention not only to the connections we have with all people and with all life, but also to the debt we owe others by respecting them and responding to their needs. The particular skill of justice is to recognize the various kinds of relationships we have with all people — friend, spouse, business partner, fellow citizen, fellow human being — and *precisely because of these relationships* to treat them fairly and honorably. There is a vision to justice that recognizes the inescapable links that bind us to others and the obligations those ties bring. Justice tells us we are bound to care for the needs of others precisely because we live in relationship with them. All the responsibilities entailed by justice stem from the fundamental fact that every human being *without exception* is linked to us and part of us; thus to give these others their due is nothing more than to recognize how much they are part of ourselves.

As a virtue, justice is both a quality of character and a rule of action. As a quality of character, justice habitually disposes us to take the needs and well-being of others into account; it describes the person who is *characteristically attentive to the good of another,* not exclusively or even primarily focused on himself. As a rule of action, justice insists that the principal element *to any genuinely moral act* is to render the debt we owe another. In this respect, justice focuses our behavior on the well-being of our neighbors. There is, of course, a justice we owe ourself and that others owe us; however, precisely because justice is the quintessential virtue governing relationships, its core energy is to direct our concern to the good of others. It is through justice that our attitudes and actions are informed by a fundamental and enduring concern for the well-being of others, including nonhuman creation. The opposite of selfishness, justice sets our will to respect, to care about, and to seek the good of another.

The special power of justice is to open our eyes to the needs and rights of others and to give us the skill to know how to respond to them fairly and wisely. Justice draws our attention to the others with whom we live, whether they be nearby or oceans away. It is the virtue which reminds us there are other centers of life we must take into account in how we think and how we live. In this respect, justice chastens egoism by reminding us that our needs and interests are not absolute because there are others and we are obliged to consider them. These others do not exist solely to serve our plans and fulfill our needs; rather their needs and interests and dreams are always relative to our own and inseparable from our own. They cannot thrive without our care and consideration, and we cannot thrive without theirs. Justice opens our eyes to see how completely our life is bound up with the lives of others.

It struggles with the selfishness which tempts us to focus on the plot of our own lives at the expense of everyone else. It calls us to look beyond ourselves to ask what the impact of our behavior, especially our way of life, is on others. Justice obliges us to balance our wants and needs with the well-being of others, and sometimes demands that we sacrifice immediate interests for the more basic needs of our neighbors. In short, the just person lives with others in mind. In his *A New American Justice*, Daniel Maguire puts this well:

> Justice is the first assault upon egoism. Egoism would say: "To me my own." Justice says, "Wait. There are other *selves*." Personal existence is a shared glory. Each of those other subjects is of great value and commands respect. The ego has a tendency to declare itself the sun and center of the universe. Justice breaks the news to the ego that there are no solar gods in the universe of persons. Justice is the attitude of mind that accepts the others — all others — as subjects in their own right. Justice asserts that one's own ego is not absolute and that one's interests are related. In the simple concession that each deserves his own, the moral self comes to grips with the reality and value of other selves. Justice is thus the elementary manifestation of the other-regarding character of moral and political existence. The alternative to justice is social disintegration because it would mean a refusal to take others seriously.[12]

Justice works for, and is built upon, the discovery of the value of other persons. In order for us to be unjust, we must convince ourselves that some people are without value; thus, we owe them nothing. Justice argues otherwise. Justice says everyone is due something because everyone matters. No one is expendable, no one can be ignored. Justice pivots on our willingness to see the inherent value and dignity of every person as a child of God fashioned in the image of God. Christian justice argues that because everyone is created in the image and likeness of God, we share a fundamental equality with one another before God. No person is more important than any other, no one more valuable or precious. Justice grows from the discovery of the inalienable worth of other persons, and testifies that because everyone has dignity, the fundamental well-being of some can never be sacrificed for the casual enhancement of others.

Thus, justice captures the indebtedness we have toward others not on account of what they have done for us or what they may have achieved, but on account of their value and worth as persons. We will be just to others only when we first have discovered (and acknowledged) their value. This is why the discovery of the value of persons both precedes and grounds the discovery of justice, or why, by contrast, we will never be just to anyone in whom we see no value. As Daniel Maguire puts it, "The move from pure egoism to justice is nothing more or less than the discovery of the value of persons, or, in the common term, the discovery of 'the sanctity of life.' "[13] But it is also why he warns that "only justice stands between us and barbarity. In this realm, when justice fails, persons perish."[14]

Justice also grows from and reflects a relational understanding of the self based on the common unity of humanity. Instead of seeing us as isolated and autonomous units of life having no connection to others except what we choose or are willing to acknowledge, justice argues that human life, from first to last, is shared life. We are not first solitary individuals who later choose to be in relationship with others; rather we are born into and constituted by webs of relationships outside of which we have no identity, indeed no life. As Maguire observes, "From conception until death, human life unfolds under the physical law that to be is to share. Our social history is etched in our genes. Everything about us is social."[15] Maguire underscores the deep interconnectedness that exists between us and others. But he also reminds us that if "everything about us is social," we owe something to others in justice because our lives are inextricably enmeshed with theirs — we are *in them* and they are *in us*.

In Christian language, a relational understanding of the self acknowledges that all of us are children of God, sisters and brothers in Christ. Traditionally the doctrine of the Mystical Body of Christ has expressed this, suggesting that all of us together form one person in Christ. We *are* this mystical body; to be human is to live as one of its members and to participate in its life. Justice is possible only when we acknowledge these bonds which exist between us and live in a way that honors them. If we are all members of one another, this means our unity is much deeper and more important than whatever may distinguish or divide us. It means none of us can be if we exclude anyone else. It means the diminishment of one is the diminishment of all. And, most of all, it means we are meant to be one, each person contributing to the well-being of others, everybody building everybody else up in justice and love.

As Dorothy Day wrote in her autobiography, *The Long Loneliness,* "I always felt the common unity of our humanity; the longing of the human heart is for this communion."[16] She reminds us that community is the truth about humanity, and it is this solidarity that justice seeks to nurture and protect. In other words, justice is impossible unless we appreciate that all men and women are our brothers and sisters, not outsiders or strangers, but members of the family of God.

What Injustice Denies

But of course this is exactly what injustice denies. Injustice shouts that all men and women are not our sisters and brothers, only some are, usually the ones most like us. Injustice shouts that most people are outsiders and strangers, clearly not members of the household of God; that is why we can ignore them and need not worry about them. If justice works to make the world one, injustice is determined to keep the world broken. If the energy of justice is for community, the malevolent power of injustice is all the violence, both subtle and strong, that divides, alienates, diminishes and destroys. The energy of injustice is against community; it works to deny the bonds which exist between us and thwart the relationships we need if everyone, not just the privileged, is to know fullness of life. Injustice fractures life by fostering the selfishness and indifference which keep us from being one. Justice testifies that we are meant to be one, and it is flagrantly denying this truth that makes injustice dehumanizing for both its perpetrators and its victims.

After the debate, Isabel is tutored in the ways of injustice. When Mr. M and the rest of the students leave the classroom, Isabel and Thami are alone. In talking with one another they begin to learn about each other's very different worlds. Isabel says her father is a chemist, that she is the rebel of the family, that English is her favorite subject, hockey her favorite sport, and that she wants to go to Rhodes University, study journalism, and be a writer. Thami responds that his parents are in Cape Town, his mother a domestic and his father a worker for the railroads. He lives with his grandmother and married sister because his parents felt it would be safer for him in a rural setting than in one of the township schools around Cape Town.

Then the conversation turns serious. When Isabel tells Thami her school years have been her "best years, happiest years," he quickly responds, "No. I won't be saying that," adding, "I don't want to leave any part of me in this classroom."[17] This surprises Isabel, but Thami explains, "School doesn't mean the same to us that it does to you." He admits he once loved school, so much that he "wanted to have school on Saturdays and Sundays" and "hated the holidays,"[18] but Isabel does not understand. She knows Thami is bright and does not grasp why he would not be as enthused about the future as she is.

Why Some Can Afford to Dream and Others Cannot

Isabel does not understand that she can have grand ambitions and grand dreams because she has been given a way of life that makes those ambitions and dreams possible. She can risk hope-filled plans and great expectations because as a well-to-do young white woman in South Africa under apartheid, everything has been designed to put those possibilities within her reach. Isabel is one of the privileged in a society tilted to favor her. She can afford promising dreams because she lives in a society where everything is structured to her advantage. But it is not that way for Thami. Somebody has to suffer for the disproportionate privileges Isabel and other white South Africans enjoy. Every unjust privilege has its victims, and Thami lets her know she encountered some of them in his classroom that afternoon. If with injustice the goods and opportunities of society are inordinately tilted toward some, they are correspondingly tilted away from others. Injustice means something is out-of-balance. Specifically, it describes a society structured to empower some and exclude many. Apartheid, for instance, guaranteed that a particular minority of South Africans shared fully in all the goods and opportunities of society, but always at the expense of a majority who were not allowed to participate at all.

The brutal unfairness of apartheid is graphically disclosed in this conversation between Isabel and Thami. In many important respects, they are the same. Both are bright, articulate, personable, and talented. Both love to learn and are stimulated by education. The difference, however, is that because Isabel is white, education will open doors for her, but no amount of study can budge doors permanently closed to Thami. Apartheid guaranteed Isabel a wonderful future, but it guaranteed Thami a desolate one. Thus, there is a way his intelligence is more a curse than a blessing. He is encouraged by Mr. M to develop his talents, but he realizes his education will take him not, like Isabel, to promising places and glittering possibilities, but only to frustration and defeat because he lives in a society where everything is prearranged to hinder him.

Thami offers a fuller account of his disillusionment at the end of act one. He stands alone, speaking only to the audience, reminiscing about his earliest days as a school boy. "Starting with the little farm school, I remember my school bells like beautiful voices calling to me all through my childhood . . . and I came running when they did," he tells us. "In junior school I was the first one at the gates every morning. I was waiting there when the caretaker came to unlock them. Oh yes! Young Thami was a very eager scholar. . . . 'A most particularly promising pupil' is how one of my school reports described me."[19] He remembers an essay he wrote when he was ten years old and still believed promising possibilities were open to him. At the time he said, "The story of my life so far has also got a very happy ending because when I am big I am going to be a doctor so that I can help my people."[20] But now, several years later, Thami admits that ambition has died.

I must bring my story up to date because there have been some changes and developments since little Thami wrote those hopeful words eight years ago. To start with I don't think I want to be a doctor anymore. That praiseworthy ambition has unfortunately died in me. It still upsets me very much when I think about the pain and suffering of my people, but I realize now that what causes most of it is not an illness that can be cured by the pills and bottles of medicine they hand out at the clinic. I don't need to go to university to learn what my people really need is a strong double-dose of that traditional old Xhosa remedy called *"Inkululeko."* Freedom. So right now I'm not sure what I want to be anymore. It's hard, you see, for us "bright young blacks" to dream about wonderful careers as doctors, or lawyers, when we keep waking up in a world which doesn't allow the majority of our people any dreams at all.[21]

Those are disturbing words. Sad words, too. Standing alone before the audience, Thami speaks a shattering and sorrowful truth: injustice finds power in bringing people to despair. Thami suffered a terrible injustice under apartheid because it denied him the possibility of having hopeful dreams about his future. A basic need of human beings is to be able to make promising plans for our lives. We must be able to dream and to plan if our spirits are not to shrivel, something Thami recognized when he said what his people needed were not pills and bottles of medicine, but a "strong double-dose" of freedom. The special wickedness of widescale injustice is that it tells people they are not worthy of grand dreams and great possibilities because they lack the dignity to deserve them. But not to be allowed to dream is not to be allowed to be human.

The pernicious strategy of systemic injustice is to make people apathetic about their own lives by convincing them they do not matter. To wake up each day in a world which denies you any dreams is to be told you are expendable, and if you hear it repeated often enough you begin to believe it. The ultimate perversity of injustice is that it subjugates people by destroying not only their self-esteem, but indeed their identity; however, this is no surprise since the aim of institutionalized injustice is to depersonalize the oppressed by convincing them they are not human at all. It is no secret that the best way to gain power over people is to strip them of their identity — to make them nonpersons — and this is always the aim of unjust systems and practices.

Alone in the classroom, Thami continues to speak. He ruefully recalls the visit of an education official to his school, a robust and confident man who worked hard to convince Thami and his friends that the future was theirs to embrace. With false enthusiasm he told them, "We want you to be major shareholders in the future of this wonderful Republic of ours."[22] But Thami does not remember much else he said that day because he was distracted "with that one word: the Future!"[23] He could not get past that single formidable word because for him the future did not conjure visions of open-ended possibilities, but memories of lies and broken promises, all designed to keep an abject people down. As much as Thami would like to have great dreams and beautiful hopes for the future, he cannot afford to believe or to trust. While Isabel grows enthused and full of hope when talk turns to the future, Thami turns tense and defensive. He hears the school official's speech not as a gospel to embrace, but as a trap of which to beware.

And not without reason. Thami is a stranger to hope because he and his people had been too often misled and deceived. He wonders if the school official thinks black South Africans are blind and stupid, that "when we walk through the streets of the white town we do not see the big houses and the beautiful gardens with their swimming pools full of laughing people, and compare it with what we've got, what we have to call home?"[24]

Thami finds the promise of a glorious future incredible because of what he sees every day. Throughout his short life he has seen his people humiliated, beaten down, and wasted by apartheid. He has seen the people he loves abused and ridiculed, fathers and mothers shamed before their children. Why should he listen to promises of opportunities and success when he knows his people are little more than beasts of burden for the privileged? Why should he be duped by pledges of hope when all around him he sees his people barely able to survive? What apartheid has told Thami day after day after day is that he and all black South Africans are owed nothing because they are worth nothing. If justice is the constant reminder that every person matters, injustice is the constant reminder that in our world many people do not. This is what every black South African was told each day. It is what every marginalized person and every marginalized group continue to feel. And it is why Thami, with pain and bitterness, says,

> I look around me in the location at the men and women who went
> out into that "wonderful future" before me. What do I see? Happy
> and contented shareholders in this exciting enterprise called the
> Republic of South Africa? No. I see a generation of tired, de-
> feated men and women crawling back to their miserable little
> *pondoks* at the end of a day's work for the white *baas* or madam.
> And those are the lucky ones. They've at least got work. Most of
> them are just sitting around wasting away their lives while they
> wait helplessly for a miracle to feed their families, a miracle that
> never comes.
>
> Those men and women are our fathers and mothers. We have
> grown up watching their humiliation. We have to live every day
> with the sight of them begging for food in this land of their birth,
> and their parents' birth ... all the way back to the first proud an-
> cestors of our people. Black people lived on this land for centuries
> before any white settler had landed![25]

What Injustice Does to the Oppressed

Tired, broken-down people, people who exhaust themselves but get
nowhere, people humiliated in their own land, and people forced to
rely on miracles because they cannot rely on justice. Thami paints a
painfully accurate picture of the harvest of injustice, and it should
come as no surprise. The strategy of injustice is simple: to assure the
prosperity of a few despite the misery of the many. With justice no
one is dominated, everyone is served, everyone is cared for, and everyone finds life. But injustice works otherwise. In an unjust situation not
everyone lives, only the unjust; the oppressed die but their deaths are
acceptable because they are not considered nearly as human as their
oppressors. In his book *Ethics and Community*, Enrique Dussel captures the undeniably sinful nature of the injustice suffered by the poor,
noting how an essential characteristic of injustice is domination of the
many by the few:

"Poor," in the biblical sense, denotes the dominated, oppressed, humiliated, instrumentalized term of the practical relationship called sin. The constitutive act of the "poor" in the Bible is not lacking goods, but *being dominated,* and this *by the sinner.* ... The "poor" are those who, in the *relationship of domination,* are the dominated, the instrumentalized, the alienated.[26]

What does being oppressed and humiliated for days, weeks, months, years — even a lifetime — do to a person? We can appreciate this if we think of how upset we are anytime we feel we have been treated unjustly even when the injustice we have suffered is slight. We have all had experiences of being treated unfairly, if only momentarily. But think what it is like to be slighted and deprived every day of your life, not in superficial or trifling matters, but in the very things which make us human: freedom, food, dignity, opportunity, education, shelter, respect. To live with such thorough and deliberate oppression is to be crushed by the violence of injustice. Crushed lives are broken lives, but they are also lives easily filled with anger and resentment over the horrors they have suffered. If it takes freedom and opportunity and respect to keep us human, oppression, servitude, cruelty, deprivation, ridicule, and abuse will work a different transformation, poisoning what is promising in a person until hearts that are meant to love and praise are poised to explode in desperate rage.

Injustice does not make people docile. Injustice nurtures violence and resentment, anger and despair, in hearts that are meant to know love and truth and justice and peace. If the powerful and the privileged are shocked by this, Mr. M asks them to imagine what it is like to be black in a country where your humanity is measured by the whiteness of your skin. Before you judge us for the anger that rages inside us, he counsels, spend a day being us. Feel what it is like to be us. Look into the faces looking at us. Know what it is like to be excluded and denied. And then listen to your frightened heart. Is it any wonder violence is enkindled there, not gentleness and hope?

Look at me! I'm sweating today. I've been sweating for a week. Why? Because one of those animals, the one called Hope, has broken loose and is looking for food. Don't be fooled by its gentle name. It is as dangerous as Hate and Despair would be if they ever managed to break out. You think I'm exaggerating? Pushing my metaphor a little too far? Then I'd like to put you inside a black skin and ask you to keep Hope alive, find food for it on these streets where our children, our loved and precious children go hungry and die of malnutrition. No, believe me, it is a dangerous animal for a black man to have prowling around in his heart.[27]

Justice demands compassion for the pain of others, but compassion is exactly what the unjust lack and cannot afford to risk. Unjust people are too self-absorbed to know someone is hurt by the way they live and too callous to care, but their obliviousness does not erase the pain suffered by the oppressed. If someone is being crushed by our selfishness and obliterated by our greed, eventually something deep inside them cries out in protest. The revolt Mr. M sees seething in the hearts of his people, especially the young, is enkindled by the selfishness and callousness of those whom injustice prospers. You cannot for long deny people all a human life requires without them eventually growing angry and desperate enough to seize it for themselves. Mr. M concludes his reflections with a warning. Time is short. If justice is not enacted to give twenty-five million black South Africans — and, indeed, all victims of injustice — what they need to live humanly and decently, the results will be disastrous not only for them, but for everyone. Sensing a bloodbath on the horizon, Mr. M warns,

> The people tease me. "Faster Mr. M" they shout to me from their front doors. "You'll be late." They think it's a funny joke. They don't know how close they are to a terrible truth.
>
> Yes! The clocks are ticking my friends. History has got a strict timetable. If we're not careful we might be remembered as the country where everybody arrived too late.[28]

Contemplating the Sad and Tragic Harvest of Injustice

Like any disease left untreated, injustice is a fatal pathology. If it is not addressed by the healing medicines of respect, freedom, opportunity, education, and employment, it grows like a cancer gone wild, destroying everything in its path. This is captured vividly in *My Children! My Africa!* In act two of the play everything starts to unravel. Thami, frustrated and disenchanted, joins a student boycott against Bantu education, marching with his peers in the streets as they are carried away in a tide of madness and violence. At the same time, Mr. M, who refuses to take part in the strike, tries to make his way to the school but is deterred by roads "blocked by policemen and soldiers with their guns ready, or Comrades building barricades."[29] Lost amidst the mayhem, Mr. M "wandered around aimlessly, helplessly, watching my world go mad and set itself on fire. Everywhere I went...overturned buses, looted bread vans, the government offices...everything burning and the children dancing around rattling boxes of matches and shouting *'Tshisa! Qhumisa! Tshisa! Qhumisa! Qhumisa!'*"[30] As if in a nightmare, Mr. M, helpless and alarmed, watches his world fall apart.

> "No Anela," I said. "This is too much now. Just stand here and close your eyes and wait until you wake up and find your world the way it was." But that didn't happen. A police car came around the corner and suddenly there were children everywhere throwing stones and tear-gas bombs falling all around and I knew that I wasn't dreaming, that I was coughing and choking and hanging on to a lamppost in the real world. No! No!
>
> Do something Anela. Do something. Stop the madness! Stop the madness.[31]

But Mr. M cannot stop the madness. Arriving at school, he frantically rings the bell, calling to students he is no longer sure are even alive, "Come to school! Come to school. Before they kill you all, come to school!"[32] And as he would on any ordinary school day, Mr. M begins by calling roll, but this time each name becomes part of a litany of lamentation to all of apartheid's victims:

> Johnny Awu, living or dead? Christopher Bandla, living or dead? Zandile Cwati, living or dead? Semphiwe Dumbuzu...Ronald Gxasheka...Noloyiso Mfundweni...Steven Gaika...Zachariah Jabavu...Thami...Thami Mbikwana...Living or dead?[33]

Then Thami enters the classroom and tells Mr. M he has been denounced as an informer, accused by the Comrades for giving names to the police. Thami warns Mr. M there is a plan to march to the school, burn it down, and kill him. Mr. M admits he did go to the police captain and gave him names of those he thought were responsible for the rioting. He tells Thami the captain offered him money for the information, but he refused it. He tries to explain to him why he went to the police. He went because he felt it was his duty to do what he could to bring an end to the madness swirling about them, the madness of arson, mob violence, and lawlessness he thought would destroy them all. But he also went because he was a teacher and he missed his students. He had dedicated his life to teaching and saw it as his one gesture of hope in a cruel, violent world.

Pondering the Roots of a Particularly Ugly Death

Moments later Mr. M goes outside and is swarmed by a mob, some of whom are his students. They beat him with an iron rod and set him on fire. A few days after his horrible death, Thami and Isabel meet. She tells Thami she has tried to understand what drove the mob to kill a man who was unquestionably good and who wanted nothing more than to help the people who killed him, but no amount of prayer and reflection can help her accept or make sense of something she finds ugly and evil and terribly sad. "All I need is someone to tell me why he was killed," she says to Thami. "What madness drove these people to kill a man who had devoted his whole life to helping them. He was such a good man, Thami! He was one of the most beautiful human beings I have ever known and his death is one of the ugliest things I have ever known."[34]

Mr. M's death may have been the quick, sudden work of a frenzied mob, but its roots go far deeper. That outburst of violence was the final flowering of an evil planted with apartheid and nurtured through years of stunted lives and frustrated dreams. It does not excuse his murder, and Isabel is right that the death of a man so beautiful in goodness is ugly and evil and horrible; however, it does help us understand the complex array of forces, circumstances, and dynamics which lay behind Mr. M's violent death. Yes, there was madness and viciousness in the mob that killed him and what they did can never be justified; but it is equally true that their violence was engendered, even encouraged, by a system of injustice deliberately designed not only to pulverize their hopes and mock their dreams, but also to leave them so desperate that they would begin killing one another. This is why we view Mr. M's murder too narrowly if we overlook the larger context out of which it was born. Thami alludes to this. He admits Mr. M's death was a tragic, stupid waste, and his blood will forever be on their hands. But will his blood be on their hands only? He asks Isabel to try to understand how such a senseless, violent deed might erupt in lives too long twisted by the demonic powers of injustice.

> Try to understand, Isabel. Try to imagine what it is like to be a black person, choking inside with rage and frustration, bitterness, and then to discover that one of your own kind is a traitor, has betrayed you to those responsible for the suffering and misery of your family, of your people. What would you do? Remember there is no magistrate or court you can drag him to and demand that he be tried for that crime. There is no justice for black people in this country other than what we make for ourselves. When you judge us for what happened in front of the school four days ago just remember that you carry a share of the responsibility for it. It is your laws that have made simple, decent black people so desperate that they turn into "mad mobs."[35]

Is Thami right? Who is the murderer here? Who is responsible? Thami argues that Mr. M was killed not only by the mob, but also by the white South African society whose laws, policies, and institutions ravaged black South Africans for so long that eventually their smoldering anger, resentment, and desperation flashed forth in acts of rage. Acts can have multiple causes, and Thami suggests there was more than one group responsible for Mr. M's death — more than one agent of the act which killed him. Yes, he was directly killed by the mob of young people angry at him for having gone to the police; however, Thami insists, his death was also the work of a violent, unjust society that transforms decent people wanting decent lives into murderous mobs. Where did Mr. M's murder begin? Did it begin with the mob who beat and burned him to death? Or can its origins be traced back even further? Is there blood on the hands of the oppressors as well? Are they completely without fault?

Isabel does not deny this, but insists it does not lessen the evil of Mr. M's death. She understands Thami's position, but it does nothing to soften her sorrow or ease her sense of absolute loss. No matter how Thami interprets Mr. M's killing, Isabel cannot overcome her conviction that his death was meaningless and absurd. "Oh, Thami, it is all so wrong! So stupid! That's what I can't take...the terrible stupidity of it. We needed him. All of us."[36]

Isabel is right. What happened in South Africa under apartheid, and continues to happen all over the world wherever injustice flourishes, is stupid and wrong, a terrible and pointless evil whose immorality is heightened because it does not have to be. Injustice is neither fate nor destiny; it is not an unavoidable fact in a fallen and sinful world. Injustice is a human creation, the handiwork of our minds and hearts. We are the agents of oppression. It is our selfishness that makes others suffer, our cruelty that makes wounded hearts cry, our greed that leaves too many dying. The world does not have to be divided between oppressors and the oppressed, between conquerors and victims, between persons and nonpersons. It is not now, and has never been, part of God's plan that some starve while others feast or that the few are lifted up while the many are crushed. God's dream for the world is not the nightmare of injustice, but the peaceable kingdom, that just and true community where the needs of every member are met and people build one another up in honor, reverence, and love.

Isabel despairs of a country destroying itself by the violence and injustice of apartheid, but as the recent history of South Africa indicates, apartheid was not a fate to which South Africans were doomed, but a sinful situation they came to repent and are hopefully committed to reversing. The same can be true wherever injustice reigns. If injustice is human beings' monument to hatred, selfishness, greed, cruelty, violence, and indifference, that monument can be taken apart brick-by-brick through actions marked by generosity, compassion, kindness, sacrifice, friendship, care, and reverence. Injustice is a *human creation,* the direct result of attitudes and actions which persistently place the self's well-being over the well-being of others. But *justice is a human creation too* and the movement from injustice to justice begins in a radical conversion of those attitudes and actions that make injustice possible. No matter how much of the world's bloody history has been characterized by violence and oppression and injustice, our hope is precisely that human beings can change and be better; indeed, through the power of our actions we can build the peaceable kingdom — what the gospel calls the reign of God — instead of a kingdom of death. Put differently, if we are willing to undergo the costly conversion necessary for justice, we can build beautiful and noble monuments instead of monuments of shame.

How Injustice Is Overcome and Justice Restored

Conversions to justice often begin in moments of hospitality, openness, and risk. Such was the case with Isabel who, on the afternoon of her debate with Thami, was received into a world so completely different from her own. After the debate she stayed behind to talk with Thami and in that conversation learned about people she had never considered before, people she had seen but never noticed, people she knew about but never really thought about, viewing them not so much as individual persons with distinct struggles and joys, but as part of the background scenery of her life.

But the day Isabel crossed the boundary separating her white world from the black world of the location, she was shocked into a different awareness. She admits that she and her friends had driven to Thami's school that afternoon feeling smug and self-righteous, thinking of themselves as altruistic yet superior, noble missionaries about to share their superiority with the unenlightened. "So off we went... myself, Renee Vermaas and Cathy Bullard, the C.G.H. Debating Team... feeling very virtuous about our 'pioneering' mission into the location," Isabel recalls. "As Renee tactfully put it: 'Shame! We must remember that English isn't their home language. So don't use too many big words and speak slowly and carefully.'"[37] For Isabel, however, presumption and arrogance faded into shock and dismay as soon as she entered Thami's classroom.

They were waiting for us in what they called Number One Class-room. Honestly, I would rate it as the most bleak, depressing, dingy classroom I have ever been in. Everything about it was gray — the cement floor, the walls, the ceiling. When I first saw it I thought to myself, how in God's name does anybody study or learn anything in here.[38]

But what Isabel remembers more than the depressing classroom is that when she went to Zolile High School it was the first time in her life she was not accepted and affirmed just because she was white. For the first time she was on equal footing with black South Africans, and if she succeeded in her debate that day it would not be because of the color of her skin, but the merits of her arguments. "When I stood up in front of those black matric pupils in Number One Classroom it was a very different story," Isabel recalls. "I wasn't at home or in my dad's shop or in my school or any of the other safe places in my life. I was in Brakwater! It was *their* school. It was *their* world. I was the outsider and I was being asked to prove myself. Standing there in front of them like that I felt . . . exposed! . . . in a way that had never happened to me before."[39]

Standing there without the protective covering of apartheid which isolated her from her sisters and brothers on the location, and for the first time uprooted from the consoling security of her world, Isabel's eyes are opened. It was the moment that turned her life around, the moment that helped her see how small and privileged and skewed her world had really been. Isabel's conversion to justice begins here:

But there they were, about forty of them, my age, mostly boys, not one welcoming smile among the lot of them. And they were studying something and very intently . . . three privileged and uncomfortable white girls, in smart uniforms, from a posh school, who had come to give them a lesson in debating. . . . Well, . . . when it was my turn to speak and I stood up and looked at those forty unsmiling faces, I suddenly realized that I hadn't prepared myself for one simple but all-important fact: they had no intention of being grateful to me. They were sitting there waiting to judge me, what I said and how I said it, on the basis of total equality. Maybe it doesn't sound like such a big thing to you, but you must understand I had never really confronted that before, and I don't just mean in debates. I mean in my life![40]

The Uprooting and Awakening in Which Justice Often Begins

From that moment on nothing would ever be quite the same for Isabel. In many respects, that afternoon at Zolile High was the start of the moral life for her, and it was certainly the beginning of her conversion to justice. None of us can be moral without being just, and we cannot be just unless we have made the discovery that something other than ourself is real.[41] As Isabel came to see, it is not an easy discovery to make because it means we must acknowledge other points of view, other ways of understanding and valuing, and other ways of experiencing life. Too, acknowledging worlds other than our own exposes some of our biases and blind spots, and helps us discover why many of our cherished opinions may be wrong and our honored practices unjust. That afternoon at Zolile High Isabel's life was uprooted as she was pulled beyond the restrictive (and unjust) confines of her own narrow world into the vastly different world of Thami and his friends. She suffered the displacement and decentering with which conversions to justice often begin. More important than her debate victory that afternoon, Isabel began to see the world more truthfully.

This is why Thomas W. Ogletree says morality is a matter of learning to be hospitable to the stranger. Our moral growth and development — indeed, the possibility of being moral at all — hinge on our willingness to welcome into our lives people very different from ourselves, especially those we initially are most tempted to dismiss. We become and remain moral by having our viewpoints and practices stretched and challenged by the perspectives of others. It is only through hospitality to all the "strangers" in our lives, whether they be the poor, people of different political or religious beliefs, people of racial and ethnic minorities, people of a sexual orientation other than our own, that we become aware of the bias and self-interest that color what we take for granted and have come to call "good." To be just in our dealings with others we need the challenge of novel perspectives, especially those of the marginalized and oppressed, and contact with people who do not share our assumptions about life, particularly people we tend to exclude precisely because they are different. For Ogletree, hospitality (and I would add humility) is preliminary to being moral and therefore just, because without it our moral reasoning is too easily limited to our immediate interests and needs. Without hospitality, what we call "goodness" and "justice" may cloak an egoism by which we assess everything in terms of our own purposes and advantages; in short, morality becomes an euphemism for personal preference and enlightened self-interest.[42]

Among Thami and his friends, Isabel's whole world is called into question. Their very presence invites her to become part of a larger and more truthful world, but the only way she can do so is if she allows her own insulated and falsifying world to break down. That afternoon in Thami's classroom was the birth of a new consciousness in Isabel. Having been lured from the comfort and safety of her own world, a world structured to teach her *not to see* lest her eyes be opened to the injustice around her, she enters the world of black South Africans and almost immediately her blindness is broken through. After that day Isabel no longer sees her world in the same way. Her vision has been changed, and because she now *sees differently* she can also begin to *live differently*.

For instance, she no longer sees the location as an embarrassing backdrop to her own world, something to be kept out of sight and ignored; rather she recognizes it as a world all its own where people work and worry, sweat and dream, hunger and hope, and do anything they can to survive. That afternoon was the start of Isabel's conversion to justice because being among Thami and his friends in their school and in their world gave her a new moral vision. And her new moral vision will lead to new ways of thinking and acting. Isabel is changed by this; she is not going to be the same, and neither are we when we cross over into the world of the other. Just think what it is like to enter another country for the first time. After such excursions into cultures and worlds that initially seem so alien to us, we do not return to our old world unchanged, and neither did Isabel. Her new awareness made her less at home in a world she had always presumed was fine.

Acknowledging the Kinship We Have with One Another in God

Not long after her debate with Thami, Isabel tells Mr. M, "I've met you and Thami and all the others and I would like to get to know you all better."[43] Wanting to know "the other" better is part of the conversion to justice too. Justice is the virtue that puts people in right relationship with one another, as well as the rest of creation. Under apartheid, or any widespread injustice, people live out-of-relationship but rationalize it by denying there is any relationship at all. For this to change they must come together, listen to one another, spend time with one another, and learn from one another; otherwise differences are viewed as threats to be feared, not blessings that will enrich. Barriers must fall as previously separate worlds unite. And in that reunion people who once were strangers or enemies must risk becoming friends; otherwise the cycles of violence and injustice cannot be broken and the history of the world will continue to be written in blood.

If the vicious energies of injustice are not to prevail, all of us must realize we were never meant to live in isolated indifference or hostility to others because all of us are sisters and brothers in God and all of us are born from the same divine love. Israelis and Palestinians must see this truth, Catholics and Protestants in Northern Ireland must see this truth, Christians and Muslims must see this truth, but *we must see and live this truth as well* if justice is to be more than a utopian dream. Justice is possible only when we acknowledge and live the radical kinship we have with one another in God. When we do, we realize all those we formerly excluded are part of us, connected to us, and one with us. And because they are one with us we are responsible for them and they are responsible for us.

And if they are sisters and brothers to us they are equal to us. Equality is heresy in our world, an often mouthed but actually unthinkable proposition, because if we truly lived what we say we believe about the equality of all men and women, our lives (and our institutions) would drastically change. Isabel, for example, tells Mr. M she has come to see black South Africans as her equals, but her mother cannot understand this; in fact, she even finds contemplating such equality to be frightening.

Our churches, our social, economic, and political institutions find it frightening as well. Equality is a frightening concept, even a revolutionary one, because if we take it seriously it will restructure our lives and our world. The inordinate privileges which come to some from injustice would have to change if we lived what we say we believe about the fundamental equality and dignity of all human beings. Injustice is possible, indeed inevitable, as long as we convince ourselves that all human beings are not equal in the eyes of God and that not all human beings have value and worth and dignity. Unjust people and unjust institutions prosper as long as there remain enough individuals who believe some people matter more than others and some people matter not at all. It is easy to be unjust if we believe many are expendable and that the dignity of the multitudes can be sacrificed for the enhancement of a few.

Why Justice Requires Imagination

Although it sounds strange to say, Isabel's conversion to justice cannot be understood apart from her keen imagination; in fact, we can even say that a good imagination is a prerequisite for justice. Why might this be? Justice demands learning to see the world truthfully, but that is not easily achieved because there are so many ways our society, culture, and institutions teach us *not to see*. The last thing the rich and powerful in South Africa wanted was to see the pain and suffering of the oppressed. The same is true wherever injustice flourishes. In patriarchal societies, for instance, men are taught not to see women as their equals in dignity and excellence. Similarly, many heterosexuals have been taught not to see their lesbian and gay sisters and brothers as truly their equals in God and, sadly, all too often the churches have endorsed these distortions. The point is that we always act according to how we see, but often our vision is so skewed that we miss what is right before our eyes, especially if what we might see would challenge us to change.

And so it is easier to look and not to see. Fantasy and self-deception are much more common than genuine moral vision, and by fantasy I mean not the exercise of a well-tuned imagination, but the chronic human tendency to manipulate reality to fit our preferences and needs. The philosopher and novelist Iris Murdoch called fantasy "the proliferation of blinding self-centered aims and images,"[44] which suggests fantasy makes everything, even other people's lives, subordinate to our interests, needs, and gratification. Apartheid was a powerful example of societal fantasy inasmuch as it was a system empowered by "blinding self-centered aims and images" and sustained by a minority's need to make their privilege and power more important than the survival of their black sisters and brothers. But societal fantasies are many, whether their malignancy be expressed in racism, sexism, ethnic and religious prejudices, homophobia, clericalism, or violence. Governments, corporations, and churches can be driven by "blinding self-centered aims and images" as easily as our own hearts.

And when they are, it shows a costly, and reprehensible, lack of imagination. The fact that injustice grows from and depends on distorted and self-centered visions is exactly why a compassionate and sympathetic imagination is indispensable for justice. Imagination is a way of seeing; more precisely, since it is guided by compassion and sympathy, the imagination sees what duller eyes customarily miss. A judicious imagination is a rare moral achievement because through it a person is able not only to perceive the plight of others more vividly, but also to project herself into their situation in order to understand better what they might be experiencing. As Martha Nussbaum notes, it is easy to neglect what we cannot imagine, and this is especially true when it comes to the pain and suffering of the poor and oppressed.[45] It is our refusal to risk imagining their predicament that allows our consciences to remain untroubled. It is our inability to try to participate imaginatively and sympathetically in their sufferings that allows our behavior to remain unchanged. The most powerful impetus for a conversion to justice is to allow ourselves to feel and partake of the suffering, oppression, and deprivation of others.

And this is what Isabel does. She enters the world of the location and looks at it not from the perspective of the privileged, but through the eyes and hearts of all those forced to live there. Instead of shutting herself off from their plight and retreating to the comfort and security of her own tidy world, she tries to imagine their situation. She projects herself into their lives and through the power of a compassionate imagination wonders what it would be like to be them. Justice requires such sensitivity of heart; it demands such rare compassion. What makes Isabel worthy of admiration is that she was courageous enough to try to see the world through the eyes of Thami and his friends. In short, she became just the day she imagined what it would be like to be them.

Cultivating justice requires vulnerability to the sufferings and afflictions of others, especially if those sufferings and afflictions are a result of our thoughtlessness and selfishness. If we are going to change from injustice to justice, our hearts must be transformed. We must open them to the pain and sorrow of those whom injustice denies and allow that pain and sorrow to transform us. This is what Isabel demonstrates the day she enters the location and really *sees,* contemplating Thami's world with "newly baptized eyes." Thrust into the center of his world, she does not turn away in fear and disgust, but takes it in, allowing the strange and unsettling world of the location to reshape her heart.

Completing the Change of Heart

The cries of all the disenfranchised of the earth call us to repentance and responsibility, and it is in these that the conversion to justice is completed. Cultivating the virtue of justice demands that we — both individuals and institutions — also repent our injustice. If the patterns and practices of our lives have done harm to others, we must acknowledge our guilt and provide restitution through acts of justice; indeed, it is the only way our journey from the vice of injustice to the virtue of justice can be completed. Enrique Dussel captures the dual elements of repentance and responsibility in the conversion to justice when he writes, "It suddenly becomes clear to us that they [the poor] have rights, and that we are guilty of their disaster and have the duty to serve them, that we carry the responsibility of their saving, their salvation, their happiness, their health, their sustenance." And, he concludes, "Awareness of our *guilt* for the catastrophe of others, our guilt for their unhappiness, upon hearing their voice, is the root and wellspring of conversion."[46]

Dussel's reflections remind us that in our conversion to justice a little guilt is a good thing. We will not commit ourselves to the strenuous work of *unlearning* unjust habits and practices, and then being apprenticed in just habits and practices, unless we first acknowledge our culpability for the diminishment and destitution of the oppressed. A genuine and lasting conversion to justice is possible only when we give evidence of a contrite heart, a heart that has confronted its sin, acknowledged its guilt, shown signs of repentance, and in sorrow and hope wants to make amends.

But being initiated into the new life of justice is hardly easy; in fact, it is endlessly challenging because it asks for a total remaking of our lives, starting with our attitudes, convictions, and values, and extending to our everyday actions and practices. Indeed, a thorough conversion to justice can make us seem a misfit in an unjust world. Johann Baptist Metz says conversions to justice entail "class treason," a betrayal of our customary way of life and "all the apparently worthwhile values" of our culture such as affluence, materialism, power, gratification, and domination. For this conversion to be adequate, Metz says, it must "strike deep into our preconceived patterns and priorities of life"[47] so that we are freed "not from [our] powerlessness but from [our] excess of power; not from [our] poverty but from [our] wealth; not from what [we] lack but from [our] form of total consumerism; not from [our] sufferings but from [our] apathy."[48] According to Metz, the conversion to justice demands rejecting an "anthropology of domination" by which we define ourselves over against others, seeking our identity by subjugating and exploiting them, and allowing domination to "become the secret regulating principle of all interpersonal relationships."[49]

Domination is "the secret regulating principle" behind so many of the institutions, structures, and practices of our world, and its violence continues to kill. Instead of an anthropology of domination, we are to practice, Metz suggests, such "non-dominating human virtues" as justice and friendliness, gratitude and generosity, sympathy and tenderness, forgiveness and mercy, kindness and compassion. The revolution of justice aims at nothing less than a total interruption and radical readjustment of our lives and our world. It is not a tidy, cosmetic conversion that skims the surface of our lives, but a powerful rebellion against everything that brings undue harm, and too much death, to others. "We Christians possess a central word for this: conversion, the change of hearts," Metz writes. "Such a conversion . . . goes through people like a shock, reaching down into the direction their lives are taking, into their established systems of needs and desires. It damages and disrupts our immediate self-interest and aims at a fundamental reorganization of our habitual way of life."[50] As Metz makes clear, the liberation of justice is twofold: the oppressed are liberated from their oppression, and the oppressors are liberated from their sin.

A Timely Promise and a Sign of Hope

My Children! My Africa! ends with a young South African woman making a promise to a dead South African man. Isabel drives to the top of the Wapadsberg Pass, a place that was special to Mr. M because it was on that hilltop that he first was inspired to devote his life to teaching. Isabel goes there to pay her respects to Mr. M, but not in the usual way of bringing flowers, laying them on his grave, and then going on with the rest of her life. Isabel will honor the memory of Mr. M in another way: She will make him a promise. She promises Mr. M that she will not become another statistic to the tragedy of apartheid by perpetuating the twisted attitudes and malicious practices that made it possible. To honor the memory of the man who more than anyone had changed her life, and to insure that Mr. M did not die in vain, she commits herself to rise above the waste and madness of apartheid by becoming a woman of truthfulness, courage, justice, and nobility. Through Isabel's pledge, Mr. M's death, though tragic, is not without meaning because the dream of hope and justice for which he lived, and on account of which he died, will continue to live through her.

And so in the closing scene of *My Children! My Africa!* black South Africa and white South Africa come together in this young woman who speaks of herself neither as stranger nor enemy to Mr. M, but as one of his "children," a true member of his family. It is a scene of healing and reconciliation, of community restored, and of the triumph of goodness and courage and justice and love over the sick and divisive powers of hate, falsehood, injustice, and fear. It is also a compelling scene of hope. To the cynics, one woman's pledge to honor the memory of a just and good man may seem a trifling gesture, perhaps even folly. But that is because there is nothing more threatening to oppressors than a single dreamer who believes the world can be other than it is.

In this chapter we have considered the meaning and importance of justice, the terrible, inexcusable evil wrought by injustice, and what is required if injustice is to be overcome and justice restored. Perhaps most importantly, we suggested that a just society is impossible without people of compassionate imagination, people willing to envision both the plight of the world's victims and how our own lives must be altered for justice to be achieved. There is no shortage of literary works that have explored the harm done by injustice and the often heroic character of people committed to justice. Here are a few suggestions:

Algren, Nelson, *The Man with the Golden Arm*
Banks, Russell, *Cloudsplitter*
———, *Continental Drift*
Dickens, Charles, *A Tale of Two Cities*
———, *Hard Times*
Hegi, Ursula, *Stones from the River*
Keneally, Thomas, *Schindler's List*
Kennedy, William, *Ironweed*
MacMillan, Ian, *Orbit of Darkness*
Mason, Bobbie Ann, *In Country*
Melville, Herman, *Billy Budd*
Paton, Alan, *Cry, The Beloved Country*
Prejean, Helen, *Dead Man Walking*
Shakespeare, William, *Measure for Measure*
———, *Winter's Tale*
Sinclair, Upton, *The Jungle*
Spark, Muriel, *The Prime of Miss Jean Brodie*
Steinbeck, John, *The Grapes of Wrath*
Styron, William, *The Confessions of Nat Turner*
Twain, Mark, *The Adventures of Huckleberry Finn*
Uris, Leon, *Mila 18*
———, *Trinity*
Wiesel, Elie, *Night*
Wolfe, Tom, *A Man in Full*
Wright, Richard, *Black Boy*.

Notes

1. Athol Fugard, *My Children! My Africa!* (New York: Theatre Communications Group, Inc., 1989), 68. Subsequent page references to the play refer to this a edition only. Different editions, of course, will have different page references.

2. Fugard, 68. 3. Fugard, 68–69. 4. Fugard, 69. 5. Fugard, 69.

6. Johann Baptist Metz, *The Emergent Church*, trans. Peter Mann (New York: Crossroad, 1981), 61.

7. Fugard, 5–6. 8. Fugard, 3. 9. Fugard, 5. 10. Fugard, 7. 11. Fugard, 7.

12. Daniel C. Maguire, *A New American Justice* (Minneapolis: Winston Press, 1980), 58. 13. Ibid., 58. 14. Ibid., 59. 15. Ibid., 77.

16. Dorothy Day, *The Long Loneliness* (New York: Curtis Books, 1952), 31.

17. Fugard, 12. 18. Fugard, 12. 19. Fugard, 46. 20. Fugard, 47. 21. Fugard, 47. 22. Fugard, 48. 23. Fugard, 49. 24. Fugard, 49. 25. Fugard, 49.

26. Enrique Dussel, *Ethics and Community*, trans. Robert R. Barr (Maryknoll, N.Y.: Orbis Books, 1988), 22.

27. Fugard, 27–28. 28. Fugard, 29. 29. Fugard, 61. 30. Fugard, 61. 31. Fugard, 61–62. 32. Fugard, 62. 33. Fugard, 62. 34. Fugard, 71–72. 35. Fugard, 74. 36. Fugard, 75. 37. Fugard, 16. 38. Fugard, 16. 39. Fugard, 17. 40. Fugard, 16.

41. For further development of this point, see Paul J. Wadell, *Friendship and the Moral Life* (Notre Dame, Ind.: University of Notre Dame Press, 1989), 142–48.

42. See Thomas W. Ogletree, *Hospitality to the Stranger* (Philadelphia: Fortress Press, 1985), 35.

43. Fugard, 22.

44. Iris Murdoch, "On 'God' and 'Good,'" in *The Sovereignty of Goodness* (London: Routledge & Kegan Paul, 1970), 67.

45. Martha C. Nussbaum, *Poetic Justice: The Literary Imagination and Public Life* (Boston: Beacon Press, 1995), 91.

46. Dussel, *Ethics and Community*, 39.

47. Metz, *The Emergent Church*, 15. 48. Ibid., 72. 49. Ibid., 35. 50. Ibid., 43.

CHAPTER FIVE

FORGIVENESS

Redeeming the Things We Can Never Undo

H OW DOES LIFE GO ON? We have all met people who have been
dead their whole lives because they were not able or willing to
break free from hurts suffered or inflicted. It is as if they died inside,
as if something life-robbing and malicious had taken possession of
their souls and kept them from being free. There is nothing more
frightening than to realize there are things a person can do or have
done to them that are so devastating and wounding it makes them feel
they are dead inside and cannot be resurrected.

This is why forgiveness and reconciliation are so important. There
are so many things that come between us and life: hurts and
disappointments, broken relationships and failed marriages, terrible
mistakes and everyday thoughtlessness, petty jealousies and unspoken
resentments. We either deal with these obstacles to life through forgiveness and reconciliation, or we fall under the control of smoldering
anger, unhealed hurt, painful regrets, crippling guilt, or memories that
continue to bleed. All of us know this. If we are not able to forgive
or to be forgiven, something much more important is lost: without
forgiveness we cut ourselves off from life.

Forgiveness is the shape love takes before the hurts and bruises of
life. Life breaks down in moments of thoughtlessness, through careless remarks, in silly but painful misunderstandings. In our life together
forgiveness is a love frequently demanded of us because inevitably we
hurt one another, especially the people we hold most dear, and when
this happens we must learn how to *grow together* beyond hurt to a healing. Forgiveness is indispensable to any human life; in fact, forgiveness

141

is what holds life together and enables us, *despite everything,* to go on in hope.

Life is an ongoing movement beyond hurt to reconciliation, beyond fracture and brokenness to healing, beyond division and animosity to peace. We have to learn how to forgive one another and to be forgiven because without forgiveness we are cut off from life and cut off from one another, destined to live out our years in bitterness, resentment, and unbearable loneliness. Without forgiveness life dead ends in despair.

And so we must be able to start over. We must be able to pick up the pieces and begin again. We must be able to move through the hurts and failures and disappointments of life to healing and hope. This is what Christianity is all about. Christianity is the religion of second chances and new beginnings. It is all about moving from death back to life so that we are not held bound by the pains and hurts and failures of our past; indeed, the special power of forgiveness is to free us from a painful past so that we can know a hopeful future.

But it is also something more. As Doris Donnelly points out in her book *Learning to Forgive,* forgiveness is a way to be innovative and creative about the failures and mistakes of our lives because forgiveness means "that the decisions of human life, even when they turn out badly, are not above repair."[1] That is the great hope on which all of us depend. We need a way to deal with mistakes, errors, sins, and regrets if all our failures are not to stand in the way of life and continue to define us. When we sin grievously we need to be released from our transgressions lest we die in them. There has to be a route to recovery from all the things which bring us shame and sorrow; otherwise our life is nothing more than what we have come to regret and sin, not grace, has the final word. Anyone who has ever sinned or been sinned against knows there has to be a way we can recover the past in hope, and that is the special grace of forgiveness. The distinctive gift of forgiveness is to make redeemable a past that may not be erasable.

This is what Ian Bedloe discovers in Anne Tyler's *Saint Maybe,* the novel on which we shall focus our discussion of forgiveness. Ian is the second son of the Bedloe family of Baltimore, a motley, eccentric tribe of which Tyler writes, "They were never just the Bedloes, but the Bedloe *family,* Waverly Street's version of the ideal, apple-pie household: two amiable parents, three good-looking children, a dog, a cat, a scattering of goldfish."[2] And Ian? Ian was "was a medium kind of guy, all in all."[3] And he was a good guy too, generally a thoughtful, considerate person more or less attuned to others. But like a lot of generally good people, Ian's actions sometimes wreaked harm he never intended, in one instance catastrophically. With a single miscalculation, his life was forever changed, and Ian was forced to reckon with consequences he did not foresee and would never have chosen. Either he finds a way to confront and move beyond a grievous mistake that makes him feel awesomely guilty, or he will be incapacitated by failure and start to die inside. If Ian Bedloe is to live again he must break free of the debilitating power of guilt by embracing the liberating power of forgiveness.

Saint Maybe is a grammar in what it means for the frail and fallen to be forgiven. In this it has an extraordinary message of hope; however, it also carries an unsettling message because even though it promises nothing in life is beyond repair, it equally insists that forgiveness is a rigorous grace that involves nothing less than the reconstruction of our identity, and in this respect it flies in the face of contemporary notions of cheap and easy forgiveness. For Anne Tyler, Ian Bedloe and all the rest of us can be forgiven, but only if we realize forgiveness is both a gift and a task, a gracious invitation and a daunting responsibility; indeed, Christian forgiveness demands nothing less than being apprenticed into a new way of life in which destructive habits are slowly unlearned and gracious practices are joyfully embraced.

Ian has to learn the *craft of forgiveness*. He has to understand that forgiveness is not weakness but the most powerful force of all because forgiveness frees us to deal with our lives in hope; indeed, as *Saint Maybe* testifies, forgiveness is a *path to new life*. It is truly the most creative and innovative way of life possible because it frees us to go on not by denying our past or even by necessarily forgetting it, but by reinterpreting the past in truthfulness and hope.

But forgiveness is not so much a single act as a *process* whose goal is to teach us to live *a forgiven and forgiving life*. Living a forgiven and forgiving life — a life of gracious and heartfelt reconciliation — is precisely what Christianity is about. And so in this chapter we shall explore the contours of forgiveness by watching how this grace unfolds in the life of Ian Bedloe. We shall trace the path of forgiveness by considering four points: (1) when good intentions go awry; (2) the need for forgiveness and how it begins; (3) why forgiveness is participation in a new way of life; and (4) why the essence of forgiveness is living into a gift.

When Good Intentions Go Awry

Saint Maybe begins the spring Ian's older brother, Danny, falls in love with Lucy Dean, a waitress at the Fill 'Er Up Cafe. Lucy has two children from a failed marriage, a six-year-old girl named Agatha and a three-year-old son named Thomas. Lucy and Danny get married and seven months later, on Ian's birthday, Lucy gives birth to Daphne, causing Ian to wonder if Daphne is really Danny's child.

Lucy asks Ian to baby-sit some afternoons so she can go walking. Ian enjoys being with the children but grows suspicious. He thinks Lucy is meeting another man, not going for a walk. One day when Lucy comes home wearing a beautiful new dress, Ian is convinced the dress is a gift from a lover and vows never to sit for Lucy again.

But his mother interferes. The following Saturday Ian is to have dinner at his girlfriend Cicely's home. He is more than a little excited because Cicely's parents will be gone overnight and this meant "that after her brother went to bed, Cicely and Ian would be just like married people, all alone downstairs or maybe even upstairs in her bedroom with the door locked. They didn't discuss the possibilities in so many words, but Ian got the feeling that Cicely was aware of them."[4] In the meantime, however, Ian's mother, Bee, volunteers him to baby-sit Agatha, Thomas, and Daphne. Danny is going to Bucky Hargrove's stag party and Lucy says she is meeting her friend Dot, a waitress at the Fill 'Er Up Cafe, for a drink, although Ian does not believe her.

Angry and resentful that his mother had meddled with his plans, Ian trods over to Lucy's and spends the evening burping Daphne and playing Parcheesi and Old Maid with Agatha and Thomas. Lucy had promised to be home by 8:30, the hour Ian is to be at Cicely's, but by 9:15 she has yet to appear. An hour or so later, Ian hears someone approaching the door. Certain it is Lucy, he is poised for attack, ready to tell her exactly how she has spoiled his evening. But when the door opens it is not Lucy who is standing there, but Danny. Exasperated, Ian tells Danny he was due at Cicely's hours ago and needs him *now* to take him first to home and then to Cicely's. When Danny asks about the kids, Ian says they will be all right by themselves for a few minutes. As they pulled away, "Ian tapped a foot against the floorboards. He felt commanding and energetic, charged up by righteous anger."[5]

Ian feels the victim, the wronged one, and so he wants to shock, even to hurt, Danny a little as much as he wants to get back at Lucy. His anger prompts him to do something that forever alters his life. Certain his suspicions about Lucy are right and angry at having his once promising evening ruined, Ian tells Danny what he is sure is the truth. In one grand outburst he exclaims,

> "Goddamnit, Danny, are you blind?" Ian shouted.
>
> Danny's eyes widened and he looked frantically in all directions. "Blind?" he asked. "What?"
>
> "She's out more often than she's in! Don't you ever wonder who she's with?"
>
> "Why, no, I..."
>
> "And how about that baby?"
>
> "Baby?"
>
> "Premature baby? Get serious. Premature baby with dimples?"
>
> Danny opened his mouth.
>
> "Two months early and breathing on her own, no incubator, no problems?"
>
> "She was" —
>
> "She was somebody else's," Ian said.
>
> "Come again?"
>
> "I just want to know how long you intend to be a fall guy," Ian said.
>
> Danny turned onto Waverly and drew up in front of the house. He cut the engine and looked over at Ian. He seemed entirely sober now. He said, "What are you trying to tell me, Ian?"

"She's out all afternoon any time she can get a sitter," Ian said. "She comes back perfumed and laughing and wearing clothes she can't afford. That white knit dress. Haven't you ever seen her white dress? Where'd she get it? How'd she pay for it? How come she married you quick as a flash and then had a baby just seven months later? . . ."

Danny started rubbing his right temple with his fingertips. When it didn't seem he meant to say anything further, Ian got out of the car.[6]

Ian runs into the house not thinking of how disturbed Danny might be, but of "the biggest night of his life" with Cicely, which is why what happens next shocks him. While in the bathroom he hears an engine roar. Peeking out the window, he sees it is Danny's Chevrolet. "The headlights were two yellow ribbons swinging away from the curb. The car took off abruptly, peeling rubber," Tyler writes. "Ian dropped the curtain. He turned to confront his own stunned face in the mirror."[7] Instantly Ian realized his impetuous act — an act that began with nothing more than the desire to inflict a little revenge — had spun out of control.

> Near the stone wall at the end of the block the brakes should have squealed, but instead the roaring sound grew louder. It grew until something had to happen, and then there was a gigantic, explosive, complicated crash and then a delicate tinkle and then silence. Ian went on staring into his own eyes. He couldn't seem to look away. He couldn't even blink, couldn't move, because once he moved then time would start rolling forward again, and he already knew that nothing in his life would ever be the same.[8]

When Our Actions Take Unforeseen Directions

A single impetuous deed ends one life and forever rearranges several others. It never occurred to Ian that Danny would respond as he did. He expected his brother to be angry and to confront Lucy, not to drive full-speed into a cemetery wall at the end of the street. He thought his encounter, besides inflicting a little revenge, would rectify a presumed injustice, not lead to something as awful and terrible and irreversible as his brother's death. What Ian thought would punish Lucy and enlighten Danny instead prompted his brother to take his own life.

Time, frozen in that instant of Ian's awful realization, starts rolling again. But for Ian it is a shockingly different time, a numbingly new epoch marking off decidedly different chapters of his life. Nothing will ever be the same for Ian Bedloe because forces his act brought to life took a direction completely unforeseen and unexpected, but one Ian is powerless to stop. An act he had begun with one set of intentions takes on a life of its own and rushes toward consequences he neither desired nor thought possible. Here is an eighteen-year-old likable boy whose resentment at being inconvenienced leaves him a character in a tragedy he had no intention of bringing about, but can never erase. On what was to be (and in ways always will be) "the biggest night of his life," he who intended to undo a perceived injustice against his brother (as well as voice his own anger and frustration) finds himself the initial instigator of something as final and irreversible as death.

Ian's predicament helps us appreciate the complex, and often murky, connection between our actions and their consequences. His plight counsels us to be prudent, to reckon carefully and even cautiously the possible outcomes of our actions, especially when we risk being blinded by anger and self-righteousness. Precisely because consequences can be so incalculable, moral responsibility demands that prior to acting we take into account how our actions might go awry, and especially how they might deleteriously influence the behavior of others. We are inclined to place undue confidence in the possible good results of our behavior, but Ian's tragedy illustrates how costly this misplaced confidence can be. The danger of rash, impetuous behavior is that it neglects the careful scrutiny and reflective assessment that must be part of a genuinely prudent, and therefore moral, act The life of an action does not always coincide with our intentions, but the unintended repercussions of our behavior can be not only much more enduring than the intended consequences, but also of considerably greater moral significance. If this is true, moral responsibility requires that we take whatever time is necessary to scrutinize the motives and intentions at work in our actions, and also to reflect on their possible outcomes, especially in regard to others.

But this is precisely what Ian failed to do. His action is rash and impulsive (not uncommon for a frustrated adolescent), but also morally skewed. No matter how we assess Ian's responsibility for all that unraveled in the aftermath of his confrontation with Danny, it is at least clear that he was negligent. For instance, he never took time to determine whether his judgments of Lucy were correct. He *presumed* she was unfaithful to Danny, he *presumed* she was seeing another man, and he *presumed* Daphne was not Danny's child. But he was not sure. He interprets everything about Lucy to confirm those conclusions, but he never stops to consider whether there might be other possibilities; he never questions his assumptions.

And often neither do we. Like Ian, our judgments about people can be wrong, especially when we want to see them in an unfavorable light. Our suspicions about others can fool us, leading us to misread what might actually be happening in ways we never suspect, but in ways that can be terribly unjust. Ian's outburst to Danny is in response to what he perceives Lucy to be doing, but he does not recognize how often our perceptions can be wrong. Maybe Lucy really did meet Dot that evening.

But there are other ways Ian was negligent. Even though Ian has a right to be angry with his mother for volunteering him to baby-sit and with Lucy and Danny for being late, his anger is also dangerous because it leads him to act both rashly and vindictively. However justified, Ian's anger blinds him; in every sense of the word, his anger gets the best of him. He is so carried away with resentment that he does not think about what he plans to do and the consequences it might have.

Remember what happened that evening. When Ian drops the bombshell of his suspicions on Danny, he doesn't stop to consider the impact of what he says on his brother; he is so focused on his anger and his desire for revenge that he does not read the situation carefully. First of all, Danny does not suspect Lucy of anything. Second, Danny's been drinking and the effect of alcohol will surely color both how he hears Ian's attack and how he responds to it. But Ian charges ahead letting all his suspicions spill out, never considering how his revelation might be affecting his brother. Third, once Ian has voiced his suspicions and enacted a little revenge on Danny and Lucy for spoiling his evening, he thinks that is the end of the matter. He feels better because he has hurt the ones who have hurt him, but he does not consider how Danny might be feeling or how his ill-timed blast might ricochet in Danny's life.

Ian miscalculated the impact of his action. But how responsible is he? Should he be responsible for an act which led to consequences he never intended? Is there a way Ian has to claim ownership of what happened even though he did not directly cause his brother's death? Assessing responsibility for an action is not always easy because in a chain of actions it is hard to determine where one person's act ends and another's begins. Exactly where did the chain of events leading to Danny's death begin? With Ian's mother Bee volunteering him to baby-sit? With Lucy failing to come home on time? With Danny's drinking? With Ian's encounter? Surely Danny could have reacted differently. He could have been angry with Ian for accusing Lucy of unfaithfulness and refused to believe him; after all, he had no reasons to suspect her of infidelity. He could have thought of the children and returned home to be with them. He could have calmed down and later talked to Lucy about Ian's charges. He could have done many things other than take his own life, and that is the decisive point. Danny took his own life, not Ian. It was Danny who drove into the cemetery wall, Danny who opted for suicide.

But this does not exculpate Ian. Ian cannot be absolved of all responsibility because had he acted differently Danny would still be alive. What Ian lacked was a healthy dose of prudent restraint. Prudent restraint is not an anxious caution that leaves us fearful and indecisive, but a caution that alerts us to the mix of factors that might be influencing our behavior and of the possible range of repercussions our behavior can have, both foreseen and unforeseen. We are *obliged* to be circumspect, which means we must consider the various dynamics at work in our actions (our moods, our feelings, our biases and prejudices, our past, our fears), the significant circumstances surrounding and influencing our actions, and the potential results. In order to be morally responsible and good, we must do what Ian failed to do: we must carefully consider what is moving us to act, we must carefully consider the manner in which we are planning to act, and we must carefully consider the possible consequences of our act, especially how they might negatively impact others. If not, we remain moral adolescents, careless people who walk through life with the best of intentions, but who are liable to do all kinds of harm.

How Lucy Falls from Hope

Danny's life is over, but the lives of everyone connected to him were permanently altered too, especially Lucy's. With Danny's death, Lucy's life caves in. Devastated by her loss, overwhelmed by caring for and raising her children, financial worries, and uncertainty about the future, Lucy spends her days napping and her nights worrying. Swimming in the darkness of depression, she nurses her sorrow with alcohol, pills, and sleep, telling the children "if they would just let her be she would stay in bed from spring till fall, sleeping away this whole hot, muggy summer."[9]

This leaves the three children on their own. Agatha, only seven years old, becomes mother to Thomas and Daphne. The "adult" of the household, she fixes Daphne's bottle, feeds her, and clumsily tries to change her diaper. She is the one who reassures Thomas, answers his questions, and tells him stories at night. And she becomes mother, nurse, and confidante to Lucy, a woman whose sorrow and loss have rendered her an invalid, someone so dazed and withdrawn that she has little sense of what is happening around her. We see this the day Ian and his mother visit. Shocked by what she sees, Mrs. Bedloe asks Agatha about her mother. Agatha tells her, "If you wrap her in a blanket, she can walk pretty good. Stir coffee into her Co-Cola and make her drink it and then hold her hand; she can walk anywhere you want her to."[10]

Lucy's life is shutting down. She slides deeper and deeper into a depression and cannot seem to climb her way out. No wonder. When Danny dies she is only twenty-five, has little education or work experience, and feels wasted by a life in which much more has gone wrong than right, especially in her relationships with men. When Lucy was first married, she lived in the country in a small trailer; but when Thomas was a baby her husband divorced her. Later she was courted by Mr. Belling, a man who gave Lucy presents and the children money, but whom neither Agatha nor Thomas liked. Hoping to marry Mr. Belling, Lucy moved the family to Baltimore, only to discover he was already married. Then she met Danny, and Agatha and Thomas could sense their mother's renewed hope. "She acted more like her old self once she met Danny. On her wedding day she said it was *all* of them's wedding day. She gave Agatha a little pink rose from her bridal bouquet."[11]

But the rose quickly lost its bloom. After Danny died, Lucy tried to put the pieces of her life back together. Tired of being a waitress at the Fill 'Er Up Cafe, she decides to be a secretary in a fancy law firm. But she can't type, doesn't have a typewriter, and can't afford secretarial school. So one afternoon with Agatha, Thomas, and Daphne in tow, she sets out for Rumford & Son's Office Equipment on Govans Road, not to buy a typewriter she could not afford, but to see if they would let her practice on a typewriter there. She explains to "a lady with squiggly hair" that "she wanted to sit at a desk for just exactly twelve days and teach herself out of a book called *Touch Typing in Twelve Easy Lessons,* and she promised that all three children would be as quiet as mice," but the lady with squiggly hair tells her, "Hon, this is not a secretarial college."[12] Fearing that another door would close before she could even try to open it, Lucy explodes, "Well, don't you think I know that? . . . But how do you suppose I could manage a *real* secretarial college? How do you expect me to pay? Who would watch my children? . . . This is all I've got to go on, don't you understand? I need to find a job of some kind, I need to find employment!"[13]

Overhearing the squabble, Mr. Rumford comes to the rescue. He suggests that Lucy rent a typewriter and take it home. Exultant at the first bit of good luck in a long time, Lucy practices with a frenzy, making her way "through the first five lessons in a single sitting."[14] The next day she buys a newspaper and scans the classifieds for secretarial jobs. Seeing dozens of them, she concludes "the problem was not finding a job but choosing which one."[15] With her confidence soaring, Lucy retreats to her bedroom and starts calling for interviews; however, after several hours on the phone, she manages just one appointment.

Nonetheless, the next morning Lucy goes to her appointment confident and assured, certain the day will end with her employed. But it doesn't turn out that way. She is back by noon and Agatha and Thomas can tell just by the way their mother walks up the front steps that she did not get the job. What might have been a minor setback to somebody else was more than Lucy could bear. Is it true God never sends us more than we can handle? Lucy's plight makes us wonder. Are some people luckier in life than others? Undoubtedly so. And is hope connected to good fortune? Sometimes it seems that way. What is clear is that this last defeat is one more than Lucy can endure. By the end of the day she is sinking into the quicksand of despair.

A Child's View of Sorrow and Loss

Lucy's life was upended by Danny's death, but so were the lives of her children, Agatha, Thomas, and Daphne. In chapter 2 of *Saint Maybe,* Anne Tyler writes from their point of view. She gives us a child's perspective of a world shattered by sorrow and loss. She shows us how attuned Thomas is to every shift in his mother's mood, to the tone of her voice or the look in her eyes, as he searches for reassurance. She records how Danny's death robs Agatha of her childhood as this little girl becomes protectress of them all. And she illustrates how much children need order and security in their lives and how frightened they become when it is gone. Tyler writes a sad and moving chronicle of how often children bear the brunt of the errors, limitations, and frailties of adults, and why they are most defenseless in the face of misfortune.

It is no surprise then that one night when Thomas asks Agatha to tell him a bedtime story he insists that it be "Hansel and Gretel," a story of two children "wandering through the woods alone and lost, holding hands, looking all around them . . . two tiny specks beneath the great dark ceiling of the forest."[16]

Why We Need Forgiveness

Ian too feels abandoned and lost, but for him it is a different kind of darkness. After Danny's death he tries to return to a normal life, but finds himself battling demons that will not go away. Their names are guilt, remorse, and shame, and Ian is in their possession. They rob him of freedom and steal any fleeting peace he may know. Ian feels the burden of a transgression. The weight of this deed which will not go away presses on his heart and controls his life. His misdeed has become his master because everywhere Ian looks he is reminded of an act that swerved out of control; consequently, a young man whose life had seemed untroubled is forced to accommodate something horrible that stands between him and life. The memory of that misbegotten night haunts him, shadowing his consciousness, visiting his dreams, playing with his sanity. Ian wants a new beginning — he keeps telling himself, "Yes, life must go on!" — but he is stuck in the disabling power of guilt, unable to move beyond shame and remorse. He cannot dislodge his sense of culpability and his growing awareness of the need for reparation and atonement.

Guilt becomes his everyday companion. Ian is absorbed in it. His life is stalled by a memory that refuses to fade. At first he tries to take up his life as it had always been, living as if nothing extraordinary had happened, but it does not work. All his efforts at normalcy are sabotaged by a memory. Danny's death lurks everywhere, shadowing every moment of every day. No matter how hard Ian tries to steer his life back to what it had been, Danny's death insists on being heard. It is as if this memory is his master, Ian its slave.

> He would see it looming in his path — something dark and stony that got in the way of every happy moment. He'd be splitting a pizza with Pig and Andrew or listening to records with Cicely and all at once it would rise up in front of him: *Danny is dead. He died. Died.*
>
> And then a thought that was even worse: *He died on purpose. He killed himself.*
>
> And finally the most horrible thought of all: *Because of what I told him.*[17]

Then Ian tries to find freedom through self-deception. He seeks solace in the thought that his predicament is not unique: doesn't everyone have some hidden, shameful secret they dare not confess? Ian reassures himself that everyone walks around with some awful guilt buried in their hearts and if they would only speak he would discover he is no different from anyone else. Isn't doing something unspeakable part of everyone's history? Tyler writes,

> Sometimes he tried to believe that everyone on earth walked around with at least one unbearable guilty secret hidden away inside. Maybe it was part of growing up. Maybe if he went and confessed to his mother she would say, "Why, sweetheart! Is that all that's bothering you? Listen, every last one of us has caused *somebody's* suicide.[18]

Battling a Guilt That Refuses to Die

But the ploy fails and the guilt remains. It does not help to have Lucy as a constant reminder of Danny's death. Seeing the change in Lucy, Ian realizes she loved his brother far more than he thought and that with his death life had gone out of her too. She was joyless and diminished, a woman defeated by too many losses and too little hope. "He noticed she was growing steadily paler, like one of his father's old Polaroid photos," Tyler writes. "He wanted to believe Danny's death hadn't touched her, but there she sat with something still and stricken in her face. Her children quarreled shrilly with Claudia's children, but Lucy just sat straight-backed, not appearing to hear, and smoothed her skirt over and over across her lap."[19]

What is worse, Ian learns Lucy really had gone out with Dot the night of Danny's death and she was late because Dot's car had broken down, not because she was with a secret boyfriend. His convictions about Lucy are challenged even further when he later discovers from Mrs. Myrdal, the woman who used to baby-sit for Lucy's children, that the skirts and scarves and blouses she would bring home from her afternoon walks were not gifts from a lover, but items Lucy was shoplifting.

All these revelations stagger Ian and augment the injustice he has done to Lucy. His guilt is compounded because his rash confrontation with Danny was based on assumptions about Lucy he now discovers were false. The certainty he had that emboldened him to confront his brother was nothing more than the blindness of self-righteousness.

His brother is dead and Lucy a widow because Ian never wondered whether his assumptions were more than fictions filtered through a bruised ego. Learning the truth, Ian "felt bruised all down the front of his body, as if he'd been kicked."[20]

The summer after Danny's death Ian goes back to work for Sid 'n' Ed's A-1 Movers, hoping to lose himself in the monotony of everyday labor, but he cannot shake the memory of his brother's death and the feeling that he must do something to make an awful wrong right. In September he leaves Baltimore for Sumner College and is glad none of his friends are going with him. He wants to be alone, removed as far as possible from any reminder of his past. He hopes a fresh start in a new setting will bring healing. If he is far enough removed from all that is familiar, Ian reasons, the memory will fade, the guilt disappear, and a new life begin. The way to deal with remorse, he believes, is to distance oneself from its source.

Still, the past from which he longs to be freed stubbornly refuses to die; in fact, it explodes thunderously into his carefully planned new life the Wednesday before Halloween. That was the day his mother phoned to say Lucy was dead, apparently from taking too many pills. Listening to his mother Ian thinks, "*Oh, God, . . . How long will I have to pay for just a handful of tossed-off words? . . . Can't we just back up and start over? Couldn't I have one more chance?*"[21] Ian is *burdened* and it is killing him. He cannot understand why something he never intended will not fade away. Couldn't he rewind the past and start over? Why is it that an act which led to consequences he never intended lives on, continuing to do damage?

Ian must discover how to find freedom in relation to something he cannot possibly change. How can he move forward when the past cannot be altered? Why is it that something he desperately wants to disown not only refuses to disappear, but keeps growing over time? Why can't the gnawing remorse he feels in his heart bring an end to a mistake Ian will grieve for the rest of his life? Ian wants to leave this terrible deed behind and get on with his life, but has no idea how this can be done. Life needs to go on for him — he must be unburdened and restored — but it will only when Ian discovers how to find freedom in relation to a tragedy he can never undo.

Discovering the Power of Forgiveness

This is the power of forgiveness. Ian wants forgiveness but he does not yet know what forgiveness involves. He wants to be absolved, pardoned, shriven, and relieved but has yet to discover that forgiveness is not a word or a single act, but the reconstitution of his life in grace, mercy, truthfulness, and joy. He cannot find healing by bypassing forgiveness. There is no other route to restoration, no other possible way he can be released from his errors in order to live again. Until he undergoes the conversion and renewal at the heart of forgiveness, Ian will be ruled by his pain. The wound which is lodged in the center of his being will not go away by Ian's wishing it, but only through the painstaking, gracious, and genuinely hopeful rehabilitation of forgiveness.

Without forgiveness he will not find new life, but every day lose a little more of it. No amount of clever strategies or carefully woven rationalizations can save him. Until he undergoes the ascesis of forgiveness everything in his life will be refracted through the prism of this pain. Such unabsolved pain debilitates. We push it down further and further, hoping suppression and denial will smother it, but there in the depths it only grows more toxic, poisoning our lives in ways we do not see. Only forgiveness can release us from the incapacitating poisons which, if left untouched, shackle the soul. As difficult as offering or receiving forgiveness might be, is there a more promising way to deal with the hurts and the pains, the sins and the errors of life? If we are not able to forgive or to accept forgiveness, the hurts and regrets of our past become our prisons in the present. Like Ian, without forgiveness we become mired in transgressions we can never escape.

Instead of choosing life through forgiveness, we can make a shelter of our pains and seek refuge in our guilt. But when we do, these unhealed wounds and unabsolved sins do not disappear; rather they flourish and grow, each day gaining new power over us. As they did with Ian, they begin to control us, robbing us of freedom, snuffing out our hope, and crushing our joy. Unchecked by forgiveness, the wounds we inflict, as well as the wounds we suffer, become larger than life; in fact, they become our life.

What to Do with Actions That Are Not Erasable

In his extraordinary book *The Way of Suffering: A Geography of Crisis,* Jerome A. Miller suggests we sometimes want to distinguish sharply between who we are and what we have done in order to disown some of our mistakes or to distance ourselves from our failures; we do not wish to think of ourselves as people who can do, and perhaps have done, terrible things. "We would like to think we are not affected by the gravity of our wrong choices," Miller writes. "But each of them burdens us with a permanent weight which we are powerless to eliminate or diminish."[22] If we were not affected by our choices, they would be not just revisable, but erasable. If we could cancel our mistakes and make our errors disappear, it would mean actions were retractable. What Anne Tyler demonstrates powerfully through the story of Ian Bedloe is that one reason we cannot undo the wrongs we commit or distance ourselves from our mistakes is because our choices become part of us.

When we cause harm or bring sorrow and pain to others, we would prefer to think that we can discard those misdeeds as easily as a snake sheds its old skin. But no matter how much distance we would like to put between ourselves and our failures, they remain a permanent part of who we are, an unerasable moment of our history. This does not mean we cannot be forgiven and move beyond them through contrition and repentance, but it does mean that even forgiven sins remain part of who we are, vestige of a past we hope not to repeat.

As Miller suggests, there is such an indissoluble connection between our choices and our self that at no point are we ever without the choices we have made. We may and should repent some choices, but repenting does not erase them; rather it indicates the behavior we do not want to embrace in the future. This is why Ian cannot flee an act he deeply mourns. His ill-fated confrontation with Danny is not "over and done with" because it is an action, however regrettable, Ian will never be without. No matter how desperately he may try, there is no way Ian can go back to who he was before that evening. His life is changed forever because henceforth he will never *not be* the person who made that choice. In a passage of almost chilling perceptiveness, Miller describes the unbreakable connection between what we choose and who we are:

The choices we have made do not remain within us as mere relics from the part of our lives that is already finished. In fact, by choosing an act and thus irrevocably appropriating it, I make it a part of the self I will bring to every future. For us humans, the past is not something that happened to us once and is now over and done with. For in every choice we made in the past, we appropriated that moment of the past into ourselves forever. Choice is therefore always both irrevocable and unretractable, even though it is in some sense revisable. In every choice I engrave something in my self in a definitive way. We must not stop short of saying that I will never be without this choice. I am bound to it for as long as I exist as myself, even if that happens to be for all eternity; I *am* this choice, from now on. In the future I can choose to revise it but not in the sense of going back to who I was before I made it. I will never be able to be anything more than an act of contrition for the evil I have appropriated into my self.[23]

But this does not mean Ian is without hope, because choices we cannot erase can be redeemed through the power of contrition, repentance, and forgiveness. Mistakes we cannot leave behind do not need to destroy us or forever haunt us. As Miller suggests, we gain power over choices we cannot change, not by denying them, but by repenting them. It is repentance — genuine heartfelt contrition — that gives us freedom over unretractable choices. Contrition does not erase these choices, but it can transform moments of profound error into occasions of grace and growth. In this respect, error and grace are linked because to grow from our waywardness through contrition does not eliminate the sin but redeems it. The liberating power of repentance is that it teaches us we find healing not when we attempt to deny our failings, but when we learn to live with them redemptively.

Ian Meets His Second Chance

Ian's rebirth begins the night he stumbles upon a storefront church of the down-and-out. It is January 1967 and Ian has just turned nineteen. After working all day, he saunters along York Road heading home.

But his journey homeward is interrupted when he finds himself standing before the "Church of the Second Chance," a congregation aptly named for one who yearns to start over, but the last place Ian expects to find salvation and release. Pausing at the intersection, Ian sees the DON'T WALK sign. Is it a message that there's something here Ian should heed? A grace he cannot afford to miss? Turning, he heads back to the ramshackle building and enters a small room where no more than fifteen or twenty people are gathered on "plain gray metal folding chairs, the kind you'd see at a bridge game."[24]

There is not much impressive about the Church of the Second Chance. The pulpit was "an ordinary store counter. The floor was green linoleum. The lights overhead were long fluorescent tubes and one tube flickered rapidly, giving Ian the impression that he had a twitch in his eyelid."[25] And the minister, "a tall, black-haired man in a tieless white shirt and black trousers,"[26] seemed an unlikely mediator of new life. Ian noticed that his "cuffs had slipped down his forearms, and his collar...was buttoned all the way to the neck, in the fashion of those misfits who used to walk around high school with slide rules dangling from their belts."[27] Ian "had the feeling he was their first and only visitor."[28] It was a congregation of misfits, not a gathering of the polished and successful. And yet, when this ragtag bunch sang "Blessed Jesus! Blessed Jesus!" Ian was touched in a way no other church had ever touched him.

When the singing ended Reverend Emmett, the minister, invited anyone "to step forward and ask for our prayers," assuring them, "No request is too great, no request is trivial in the eyes of God our Father," a remark which made Ian think "of the plasterer who'd repaired his parents' bathroom ceiling. No JOB TOO LARGE OR TOO SMALL, his panel truck had read."[29] After one member prayed for Clarice, who was having trouble with her blood, and Lula prayed for her son who was killed in Vietnam, Ian, surprising even himself, stands and confesses,

"I used to be" — he said.

Frog in his throat. He gave a dry, fake-sounding cough.

"I used to be good," he said. "Or I used to be not bad, at least. Not evil. I just *assumed* I wasn't evil, but lately, I don't know what's happened. Everything I touch goes wrong....

"Pray for me to be good again," he told them. "Pray for me to be forgiven."[30]

The service ends with the congregation singing "Leaning on the Everlasting Arms," but it is not yet over for Ian. He is introduced to Reverend Emmett, who wastes no time asking him, "What was it that you needed forgiven?" Ian is flabbergasted that anyone would be so bold, wondering if it is even legal to inquire into a person's private prayers, and thinks of walking out; but instead, in "a voice not quite his own," he tells Reverend Emmett exactly what happened.

"I caused my brother to, um, kill himself."
Reverend Emmett gazed at him thoughtfully.
"I told him his wife was cheating on him," Ian said in a rush, "and now I'm not even sure she was. I mean I'm pretty sure she did in the past, I know I wasn't *totally* wrong, but . . . So he drove into a wall. And then his wife died of sleeping pills and I guess you could say I caused that too, more or less. . . . . ."[31]

Ian pauses, thinking the minister might come to his defense, arguing that "Lucy's death was just indirectly caused by Ian, and maybe not even that,"[32] but Reverend Emmett doesn't say a word. Ian goes on to explain about the children and how his aging parents do not seem up to caring for them. Finishing his confession, Ian asks, with the confidence of one expecting a positive response, " . . . don't you think? Don't you think I'm forgiven?" and is astonished when Reverend Emmett replies, "Goodness, no."[33] Shocked, Ian wonders if he misunderstood. He asks again, "I'm *not* forgiven?" and the minister calmly responds, "Oh, no."[34] Ian says he thought God forgave everything, and the minister agrees God does, but tells Ian forgiveness involves a lot more than just being sorry.

"But you can't just say, 'I'm sorry, God.' Why, anyone could do that much! You have to offer reparation — concrete, practical reparation, according to the rules of our church."
"But what if there isn't any reparation? What if it's something nothing will fix?"
"Well, that's where Jesus comes in, of course."
Another itchy word: Jesus. Ian averted his eyes.

"Jesus remembers how difficult life on earth can be," Reverend Emmett told him. "He helps with what you can't undo. But only after you've *tried* to undo it."[35]

Reverend Emmett suggests Ian can best *try* to undo his sin by taking care of Agatha, Thomas, and Daphne. Ian is dumbstruck. He reminds the minister that he is only nineteen and a college freshman, thinking Reverend Emmett will surely see how unreasonable it is for Ian to assume responsibility for three young children, but the minister quietly responds, "Then maybe you should drop out."[36] Ian thinks he must be joking or maybe it is some kind of test. He is also angry and more than a little perplexed. He had come to the church expecting to walk out forgiven and free and Reverend Emmett tells him he can be forgiven, but not at all in the way Ian expected. He says to the minister,

> "You're saying God would want me to give up my education. Change all my parents' plans for me and give up my education."
> "Yes, if that's what's required," Reverend Emmett said.
> "But that's crazy! I'd have to be crazy!"
> "'Let us not love in word, neither in tongue,'" Reverend Emmett said, "'but in deed and in truth.' First John three, eighteen."
> "I can't take on a bunch of kids! Who do you think I am? I'm nineteen years old!" Ian said. "What kind of cockeyed religion *is* this?"
> "It's the religion of atonement and complete forgiveness," Reverend Emmett said. "It's the religion of the Second Chance."
> Then he set the hymnals on the counter and turned to offer Ian a beatific smile. Ian thought he had never seen anyone so absolutely at peace.[37]

Why Forgiveness Begins with Confession

Ian's rebirth truly begins the night he heeds the DON'T WALK sign and turns to the Church of the Second Chance. The members of this motley congregation, whom Ian finds so bizarre, are really not all that different from himself. They too have had their lives shattered by misfortune, torn by unhealed grief, and shaken by countless things they could not control. But where they are different from Ian is that they are not afraid to confess their need not just for help, but for divine assistance. They *know* their dependence on God; indeed, they are absolutely certain they will perish without God's help, which is why they can confess their helplessness so joyfully. They are not ashamed and they are not afraid. They know who they are, frail, broken sinners who live by the mercy of God, stragglers who depend on his love. What Dietrich Bonhoeffer said is the truth of the gospel and the life of the church is vividly embodied in Reverend Emmett's oddball congregation: "All sham was ended in the presence of Christ. The misery of the sinner and the mercy of God — this was the truth of the Gospel in Jesus Christ. It was in this truth that his Church was to live."[38]

It is also the truth Ian begins to live. His first night with the Church of the Second Chance is a pivotal scene in *Saint Maybe*. It is the night Ian starts to know life again. And it is the night he *begins* to be freed from guilt and sorrow through the power of forgiveness. But it is only a beginning because as his memorable conversation with Reverend Emmett suggests, forgiveness occurs not in a single act but through a process, and the process of forgiveness begins with confession and repentance. The grip of guilt is loosened for Ian not by Reverend Emmett flattering him with instant, cheap forgiveness (a kind of fast-food version of forgiveness), but with Ian at last being able to voice what has haunted him for so long.

But he must do so truthfully and completely. What is needed is a clarity and transparency only mercy and grace can achieve. As Bonhoeffer says, the "message is liberation through truth. You can hide nothing from God. The mask you wear before men will do you no good before Him. He wants to see you as you are, He wants to be gracious to you. You do not have to go on lying to yourself and your brothers, as if you were without sin; you can dare to be a sinner."[39] Doris Donnelly adds that forgiveness can come only when our sin is first owned. "It is the specific acknowledgement of concrete acts for which we are truly sorry," she writes. "There is no room for equivocation, no place for vague generalities and disclaimers.... That kind of admission simply evades the issue."[40]

Disguises must be dropped and rationalizations ended for forgiveness to take root and to be real. *Saint Maybe* testifies that the power of forgiveness is that it can heal wounds, bring freedom, and restore life, but only if it begins in a confession that is truthful and complete. Forgiveness without truth does not free, but only adds layers of deception and denial. Pretense must be stripped away and we must, like Ian, encounter some unwelcome truths about ourselves. That night in the Church of the Second Chance he acknowledges something he had never before been able to accept: he belongs to the fellowship of all those who know they need to be forgiven, the fellowship of those who are not ashamed to admit they live from the mercy of God. Like them he needs pardon and deliverance. Like them he can live only if there is mercy and absolution. As Doris Donnelly explains, we must see the truth about ourselves for forgiveness to be real because, as with any sickness, a cure can follow only when an accurate diagnosis has first been made.

> And the issue is that I am responsible and that I have failed in my responsibility in concrete, specific acts which have to be named, just like a sickness has to be named, because the diagnosis precedes the cure and healing takes place most efficiently when the diagnosis has been accurate.[41]

If the pain in confessing comes from acknowledging unwelcome truths in ourselves, the hope and joy in confessing comes from encountering welcome truths in God. If the truth about us is that we die without mercy, the truth about God is that God is love and mercy through and through. We can let masks fall before God because God knows who we are and loves us. We can end all sham before God and open up our guarded hearts because God wants to free us from our sins and our guilt, not have us die in them. What makes the Church of the Second Chance a community of such unabashed joyfulness and indefatigable hope is that they know the truth about themselves and they know the truth about God. They don't need to waste time with disguises and lies because they see clearly who God is: the fullness and perfection of mercy and compassion and forgiveness. They can be who they are with unblushing honesty because they know who God is and let God be that for them — a healer, a comforter, a source of everlasting mercy.

What Ian discovers, and the members of the Church of the Second Chance know, is that what is most dangerous about the faults, sins, and guilt we bear is if they stand unconfessed. Confessed, we can be freed from them, but unspoken and unrepented they continue to corrode our lives. This is why Bonhoeffer says, "He who is alone with his sin is utterly alone."[42] Sin isolates and controls, it wants us, as Bonhoeffer argues, all by itself. Unconfessed sin is utterly destructive because its debilitating power is never broken by forgiveness. It dominates because it is concealed, it enslaves because it is protected from mercy. Ian's greatest peril was not his failure, but the chance that he might never confess it and be freed from it. His prayer that winter night on York Street was the start of his new life because once he uttered the first word of confession the spell of sin was broken. It was the dawn of his regeneration because confession brings openness to grace and room for new life. Put more strongly, confession is the space we need to make ourselves available to God so that God's mercy can enter and heal us. Without confession and repentance we shut ourselves off from the pardon we need if we are ever to know life again. Bonhoeffer captures well why hope and liberation live in the heart of every confession:

> Sin wants to remain unknown. It shuns the light. In the darkness of the unexpressed it poisons the whole being of a person.... In confession the light of the Gospel breaks into the darkness and seclusion of the heart. The sin must be brought into the light. The unexpressed must be openly spoken and acknowledged. All that is secret and hidden is made manifest. It is a hard struggle until the sin is openly admitted. But God breaks gates of brass and bars of iron (Ps. 107:16).[43]

To confess is to let go of the frenetic and futile attempt to pardon and heal ourselves. Ian cannot deliver himself, nor can he justify himself; those can never be his own achievements because they are gifts. His unburdening will be a gift from those who love him, God first and foremost, but also the members of the Church of the Second Chance. He wastes his energy if he tries to free himself, but he finds new life and his hope is restored if he accepts pardon and liberation as the gift of others' love. Ian needs to help himself, but there is a limit to what he can do for himself. The help he needs must come from without, principally in the love and mercy and sweet tenderness of God, but also in the care and compassion of this tiny church whose members praise God by gratefully witnessing the "second chances" they have received.

Why Forgiveness and Healing Require a Community

Thus, if forgiveness begins in confession and repentance, it continues and is sustained through a community. This is the second element to being healed and reconciled that Ian will learn through the Church of the Second Chance. Forgiveness may be eminently personal, but it is also inescapably communal. Healing and reconciliation are a communal event. This can be understood in three ways. First, forgiveness is necessarily communal because, as Ian's encounter with Reverend Emmett makes clear, we need others to help us understand and accept the full truth of our deeds, especially those dimensions we would rather leave hidden. In order to be forgiven and reconciled, we must make our lives available to others that through them we might be taught the truth about ourselves and our actions, and thus be open to pardon and new life. As L. Gregory Jones comments, "Overcoming self-deception and acquiring self-knowledge is an extremely difficult task." We need people who are not afraid to challenge us and speak the truth to us precisely because they care for us. It is through them that we more truthfully grasp who we are. "It is exceedingly difficult for people to attain objectivity about their own actions and character,"[44] Jones writes, but this can be reached through the help of those who care for us and want the best for us.

The aim of this disclosure is not to make us feel bad, but to release us. We confess our sins before others not that they may have new power over us, but that we might receive from them God's words of mercy and peace. The primary role of the community is not to hear our failures, but to be the ones through whom God's words of pardon and tenderness are conveyed. Bonhoeffer says we are to "meet one another as bringers of the message of salvation,"[45] and we do this best when the message of salvation we offer one another is mercy and forgiveness for the sins we all share. In short, the community is there the same way Christ is, not to condemn us in our sin but to offer us new life.

A second reason community is essential to forgiveness is that we need others to support us and to guide us as we make our way back to life. Nothing confessed is left behind instantly because forgiveness is less a sudden healing than a more gradual convalescence, and if this convalescence is to succeed we need the help of others. If, as Doris Donnelly says, the first step of forgiveness is owning our sin and repenting it, the second step, she suggests, is disowning it. She understands this to entail not only moving away from the sin by cultivating its opposite behavior, but also disowning the sin by handing it over to those who "are able to lift our burdens so that we no longer have to carry the weight of their guilt" alone.[46] Ian felt deliverance and release in the Church of the Second Chance because for the first time in months he was no longer carrying his burden alone. Now it was a weight he could hand over to others. No one arrives at forgiveness alone. To know full forgiveness and the first stirrings of a healing, we must yield our self-sufficiency. Forgiveness is essentially a surrender to those others, God as well as a faithful community, who alone can give us the healing and peace we can never offer ourselves.

Third, community is integral to forgiveness and restoration because we will never experience the full grace and healing of forgiveness unless others are willing to see us as being more than the mistakes we have made. A quick turn to the parable of the prodigal son (Luke 15) illustrates this. The mystery character in the parable is the miffed older brother who resents the warm homecoming that the father shows his wayward son. Perhaps the older brother has a right to be upset, but he has no right to stay that way. His younger brother cannot live the gift of forgiveness the father has given him without the cooperation of the brother he has hurt. He needs for his brother to be able to grow beyond his hurt and resentment if he, freshly forgiven, is to live a truly reconciled life.

In short, the older brother cannot continue to hold his younger brother's past against him. He cannot, by refusing to forgive, condemn his brother to his past and say he can be nothing more than a brother who made a mess of his life. His responsibility is not to condemn his brother to his past, but help him move beyond it. His responsibility is to see his brother in a much more hopeful and promising way, and the only way he can do this is to look at him through eyes of mercy and forgiveness, not eyes of anger and resentment. This is why so much of forgiveness is the work of a gracious imagination. Can we re-envision those who have hurt us so that we see them as something more than the harm they have done? Can we imagine something better, something more hopeful for them than their failures, and help them live it?

This is what the members of the Church of the Second Chance did for Ian. They saw him in a way he was not yet able to see himself. Never focusing on his failure, they saw possibilities for goodness, even holiness, in him that he could not yet imagine, and their love, kindness, patience, goodness, and humor helped him achieve it. Like the members of the Church of the Second Chance, each of us has a responsibility to help one another, including those who have harmed us, move beyond the failures, sins, and mistakes of the past in order to enter into a life of mercy and grace. Our responsibility is to help one another so we are not defined by the failures and misgivings of our past, but freed from them to live a *forgiven and forgiving life*. We cannot do this for ourselves, but we can and must do it together. The church should be this kind of community, a reconciled and reconciling community committed to helping one another live fully the forgiveness we have all received. We need to embody for one another those life-saving words of Jesus, the master of forgiveness, who said, "It is mercy I desire, not sacrifice" (Mt 9:13).

But for Ian's renewal to be complete he must die to one kind of life and learn another very different kind of life. This is never easy. It is like learning to walk anew. It is the challenge of trying to make sense of a wonderful but very different new world. Genuine forgiveness involves the reconstruction of our lives in gratitude and grace. No one can do this alone. No one can do it unaided. We need the help of God, but God reaches us through others, and in Ian's case God's love and life and mercy will come not only through his caring for the children, but also through his newly found friends, all the weird but joyous members of the Church of the Second Chance. It is in company with them that he will become a new creation.

Why Forgiveness Is Participation
in a New Way of Life

Forgiveness is a restorative event, but it demands a thorough revision in our basic approach to life. This is revealed in *Saint Maybe* the night Ian tries to explain to his befuddled parents how his new friends at the Church of the Second Chance will help him live a life of atonement. His father asks, "Ian, have you fallen into the hands of some *sect?*" Ian answers, "No,...I have merely discovered a church that makes sense to me, the same as Dober Street Presbyterian makes sense to you and Mom." When his mother objects, "Dober Street didn't ask us to abandon our entire way of life," Ian responds, "Well, maybe it should have."[47] Still not understanding, his father asks, "What sin could you possibly be guilty of that would require you to uproot your whole existence?"[48]

Should a church ask us "to uproot our entire existence"? Is this what Christianity *essentially* is, a total upheaval of one kind of life in order to take up another very different kind of life? It would seem so. In the gospels, when Jesus calls his followers they immediately cut ties with their past lives as fishermen and tax collectors in order to begin the new adventure of discipleship with him. And in the early church baptism signaled a complete break with one's past life in order to be initiated into a new community with its distinctive beliefs, practices, and traditions. To be baptized was to cross over into something new, to enter a new and very different narrative about what one's life in the world involved. The change was so dramatic that the baptized were said to "die" to one kind of life and "rise" into another very different kind of life; indeed, through the waters of baptism they became "a new creation." If Christianity is worth believing it cannot demand anything less than uprooting our existence, anything less than the total reconstruction of our lives as members in the transformed community we call church.

The novel suggests this when Ian, at the start of his new life, arranges to become an apprentice to a master craftsman, the carpenter and cabinetmaker Mr. Brandt. As an apprentice, Ian becomes a disciple to a master, and as the disciple of a master craftsman, Ian commits himself to learning the craft of cabinetmaking. Learning a craft is an apt metaphor for the Christian life. Through baptism Christians become apprentices — novices and raw beginners — in the discipline of learning the craft of a gospel life. Ian's mentor in this new life will be Reverend Emmett. It is under his guidance and through his example that Ian will slowly reconstruct his life and hopefully master the craft of a discipleship life.

And so begins the thorough reconstruction of his life. Ian leaves Sumner college, abandons old friends and ambitions, and uproots his whole life by taking on the responsibility of caring for Agatha, Thomas, and Daphne. His life is profoundly disrupted, but maybe it had to be if Ian was to be rescued and healed. As L. Gregory Jones explains, "When God breaks into the reality of human life and shows the truth of what and who people are, healing takes place. God interrupts the continuity of life in order to heal and renew that life."[49] Jones's point is that the healing cannot be separated from the interruption. Ian cannot find healing if his life goes on as before. For him to know forgiveness and peace his life must be disrupted at its roots, pulled up, rearranged, and planted anew; he had, as he put it, to begin "from scratch." Said more strongly, for Ian to experience deliverance his life must be disassembled, slowly taken apart and cleansed. Only then can it be reassembled in the form God's love intends for it. "At some point, every person must be 'converted,'" Jones explains, "in the sense that they must have their lives interrupted by God so that ... they might become the persons God created them to be."[50]

Forgiveness is a restorative event, but it demands a thorough revision in our basic approach to life; otherwise we misunderstand that forgiveness essentially is a *call to a new way of life*. Thus, the upheaval which occurs in Ian's life provides the opening necessary to begin a new and very different way of life. In this sense, disruption is the first state of a radical reorientation of our lives in hope, a reorientation so far-reaching that it involves the dismantling of one identity in order to be fashioned into another. This is why Ian sees that first night in the Church of the Second Chance as a boundary, a permanent dividing line between a past life and a new one. His conversion was like a change of citizenship, the joining of a new country with a distinctive culture and way of life. In order to live the new life of forgiveness, Ian cannot turn back. He must learn the habits and practices of this new community. He must learn to make his way in a life that at first will seem very strange to him, perhaps more foreign than friendly. And this learning, far from being a mere intellectual exercise, will involve a fundamental reshaping of himself.

The story of Ian Bedloe's rebirth demonstrates that forgiveness and reconciliation cannot be had apart from participation in a distinctively formative way of life; indeed, forgiveness comes through sharing in a way of life that is healing because it is truthful, joyous because it is re-creating. Forgiveness is the gift that comes through surrendering to a demanding but gracious way of life that redirects our behavior and reshapes our souls. In this respect, to be forgiven is to be educated into a different *habitus*, apprenticed to a distinctive way of being which brings genuine freedom and fresh new life. As Timothy Sedgwick remarks, "Forgiveness presupposes a normative way of life and, therefore, a community that is clearly formed in a new way of life."[51] Ian finds all this alongside the mismatched members of the Church of the Second Chance, the grateful community that knows we have all received mercy, that the ultimate reality is forgiving, and that everything is "gift and grace and acceptance."[52]

Why Doesn't Ian Feel Forgiven?

Ian holds nothing back. He commits himself to the Church of the Second Chance with a vengeance. He follows all the rules of the church. He never misses Sunday worship. He attends Wednesday night Prayer Meetings and faithfully participates in Good Works on Saturdays. He does all this painstakingly, yet after years of unstinting faithfulness he still does not feel forgiven. This is what troubles him most. He has done everything he was told to do to atone for his sin, but feels strangely bereft of mercy. Why does he not yet feel relieved? Has God even noticed? Doesn't the care and love he has given the children count for something? One Sunday morning while listening to the prayers of the other members of his church, Ian laments,

I've been atoning and atoning, and sometimes lately I've hated God for taking so long to forgive me. Some days I feel I'm speaking into a dead telephone. My words are knocking against a blank wall. Nothing comes back to show I've been heard.[53]

Doubts creep in. At the next Wednesday evening Prayer Meeting Ian tells Reverend Emmett he thinks his new life is a wasted life. He is tired of the Church of the Second Chance, tired of minding the children, and especially tired of seeing his life as nothing more than endless reparation for something he never intended in the first place. He cannot understand, when he has done everything the church asked of him, why the guilt and the grief remain. Why won't forgiveness visit him?

There may be several reasons. First, as Reverend Emmett reminds Ian, it all comes down "to whether a person feels ready to let go. . . . Some people prefer to hug their problems to themselves."[54] The minister, whose advice always takes Ian by surprise, suggests it really is up to Ian to decide when he is ready to let go of his burden and move on. Part of the process of forgiveness is coming to the point where we are able and willing to let go of whatever needs to be forgiven. We may not be able to do this immediately, but at some point forgiveness requires our willingness to let go of the past in order to move forward into the future.

But letting go, as the story of Ian Bedloe amply testifies, is not always easy. Sometimes we do not want to let go. The mistakes we have made or the harm we have suffered becomes so much a part of our identity — so central to how we see ourselves — that we cannot imagine ourselves without it. Other times we resist letting go because, despite what we say, we do not want to go forward. It is easier to sit with our hurts or to settle into our failures than it is to be healed and grow again.

Second, Ian has yet to feel forgiven because he thinks he is the only one who did wrong the night Danny died. When he thinks back to the night of his brother's death and everything that unfurled from it, he sees only his error, only his sin. But as Reverend Emmett counsels, there are other characters in this drama who have wronged Ian and whom he needs to forgive. Emmett tells Ian he will never feel forgiven until he forgives the two people he feels he has wronged the most, Danny and Lucy. The forgiveness he desperately wants to receive must be matched by the forgiveness he is willing to offer.

But why do Danny and Lucy need to be forgiven? And how do you forgive the dead anyway? Perhaps Reverend Emmett's point is that Danny and Lucy were just as responsible for their actions as Ian was. If Ian is responsible for being careless and thoughtless in how he voiced his suspicions to Danny, Danny is responsible for taking his own life. Danny drove the car into the cemetery wall, not Ian. And Lucy is responsible too. Even though her depression is understandable and we might not judge her harshly, she made the decision to withdraw from the children, retreat into her grief, and take her life.

And so just as Ian's actions had consequences, Danny's and Lucy's did so as well. He will never be without the consequences of their actions. He can never have the life he thought he would have because of them. What they did changed the lives of everyone around them, especially Ian's and the children's. Because of them his life took a shape and direction he never could have predicted and never would have chosen.

Some of the burden Ian feels is not the burden of guilt, but the burden of justified hurt and resentment. Ian has to name these and claim them in order to be free. All along he has focused on his own guilt over Danny's and Lucy's deaths, but never considered how the consequences of their actions have burdened him. Forgiveness has to reckon with both.

Third, and most seriously, Ian has yet to feel forgiven because he sees forgiveness as something he must earn. One of the dangers to the Church of the Second Chance is that all its rules and practices can suggest forgiveness is something we can eventually merit. This approach suggests forgiveness is a matter of rugged determination and steadfast observance of rules and laws. If we work hard enough, if we become experts at penance and sacrifice, forgiveness will not only be something we are owed, but something we have achieved through our own sweaty efforts. Ian misunderstands forgiveness. His wholehearted participation in his church tempts him to believe that God's mercy could be earned. He does not feel forgiven not because his contrition and repentance are lacking, but because he does not yet see that forgiveness is a matter not of merit but of gift. Not all the special programs of the Church of the Second Chance — like Good Works Saturdays — *can earn* Ian the forgiveness that all along has been his *for the taking*.

What It Means to Live into a Gift

There are several scenes in *Saint Maybe* which suggest this. One evening Reverend Emmett invites Ian for dinner, hoping to persuade Ian to be his successor in ministry. In reflecting on the Church of the Second Chance, Emmett tells Ian that most of the members of the church first came to him because, like Ian, they felt they had to atone for some sin; however, quite unlike Ian, they quickly "relaxed and settled in and entirely forgot about atonement."[55] Like Ian, they came to the Church of the Second Chance seeking forgiveness, but unlike Ian they soon forgot about their need for forgiveness and simply began living a forgiven and forgiving life.

Is Reverend Emmett suggesting Ian should do the same? Should he "relax" and "settle into" a forgiveness that he does not have to earn because it has been there all along? One way to interpret Emmett's observation about the other members of the Church of the Second Chance is that they have a keener understanding of the heart of Christianity than Ian. They realize being a Christian fundamentally is a matter of *settling into forgiveness*. They understand that mercy and pardon are not rewards we can earn, but gifts we are called to embrace. What Ian must realize is that he cannot and does not have to earn forgiveness because he has been forgiven from the start. God's mercy and pardon were there all along for Ian. What he needs to do is *live into that forgiveness*. His task is not to merit mercy, but to be grateful for it and live from its power.

In the Christian narrative of salvation and redemption the essential truth about forgiveness is this: forgiveness is a purely gratuitous, perfectly lavish, and absolutely unmerited gift. The Christian life *begins, not ends, with forgiveness*. We don't, as Ian thinks, work up to forgiveness, we start with it; therefore, the key question is not whether or not we are forgiven, but *what do we do with the gift?*

Ian is right that forgiveness involves a radical transformation of one's life, but what he does not realize is that a changed way of life is a *consequence* of being forgiven, not a *precondition* of forgiveness. We do not first have to change our lives and only then will we be forgiven; rather we *are forgiven* and because of that forgiveness we are empowered to live a new life. Again, the question is not whether we have been forgiven, but what should our lives look like *on the other side of forgiveness?* Now that we are forgiven, what does it mean to live a forgiven and forgiving life?

At the very least, it should be a life characterized by graciousness and gratitude, a life characterized by joy and new freedom, but perhaps especially a life characterized by the same mercy and forgiveness we have received. Forgiveness is a gift entrusted to us, a gift we are called to care for and develop, and it is a gift we are given not so that we can repeat the mistakes and errors of our past, but that we can reconstruct our lives in truthfulness, freedom, and grace. Living a forgiven and forgiving life means learning new attitudes, new values, new dispositions, and new virtues. But it also means *unlearning* the very attitudes, values, habits, and practices that led us to harm ourselves and others in the first place. As we stressed before, forgiveness is not a liberation that allows us to forget the past or erase it, but a gift which transforms our life and enables us to redeem the past in hope. And our past truly is redeemed in hope because through forgiveness our lives are incorporated into God's narrative of redemption; indeed, because of Christ's death and resurrection, our lives become part of a story of pardon and grace.

A Gift from a Gift-Giving God

Eventually Ian sees this. Eventually he comes to understand the giftedness of forgiveness. Near the end of the novel when Ian, now in his early forties, is talking with Agatha's husband Stuart, he tells him about what keeps him awake at night.

> "Sometimes I have this insomnia. I fall asleep just fine but then an hour or so later I wake up, and that's when the troublesome thoughts move in. You know? Things I did wrong, things I said wrong, mistakes I want to take back. And I always wonder, 'If I didn't have Someone to turn this all over to, how would I get through this? How do other people get through it?' Because I'm surely not the only one, am I?"[56]

Ian's reflection testifies that for human beings the heart of forgiveness is surrender, surrender to a mercy and love deep and faithful and enduring enough to absorb all our transgressions, all our mistakes, all our burdens, all our hurts, all our losses, and all our regrets. Ian's question is apt: How could any of us go on if there were not Someone to whom we could hand over our burdens and surrender our sins? How could we move forward in hope if there did not exist in God a mercy and compassion in which all our errors and all our waywardness could be redeemed? If the Cross of Christ means anything it means life begins with a gift, is sustained by a gift, and is fulfilled in a gift. From first to last everything is gift, everything is mercy, everything is grace. Thus, forgiveness means exactly what it says: forgiveness is *a gift-for-us.* It is a gift to live, a gift to enter into, a gift to embrace.

And it is a gift rooted in the very nature of a gift-giving God. Doris Donnelly says all of us wonder and hope that "there really does exist someone who can forgive so radically that it actually alters the shape of reality."[57] Such is the case with God. God's forgiving love alters the shape of reality inasmuch as it transforms the failures, hurts, omissions, and evil in our lives into potential sources for goodness and new life. Without God's mercy Ian's misdeed would forever endure; but the message of the gospels, and one Christ embodies, is that thanks to the radically innovative mercy of God, all things can be made new. It is not just that even the most egregious failures of our lives can be redeemed and our deepest hurts healed, but that with God's mercy and forgiveness all things can be re-created, everything broken and shattered can be restored.

What Are We to Make of Ian's Life?

We do not always see ourselves as other people see us. Throughout *Saint Maybe* Ian has focused so much on his shortcomings that he is scarcely aware of his goodness. And he has been so attentive to the failures of his past life that he does not see how for years he had been living a new life. In raising and caring for Agatha, Thomas, and Daphne, Ian had been living a forgiven and forgiving life. It was he who helped them with their homework, guided them through adolescence, and was always there when they needed him.

At the end of the novel Agatha, Thomas, and Daphne are all adults. In one scene they are together again in Baltimore and Agatha and Thomas recall the time they had the flu and the only thing they were hungry for was some of Ian's mother's "Hearts-of-Palm" dish. Ian too was sick, but he got up, drove to the grocery, and brought Agatha and Thomas what they wanted.

Ian doesn't remember any of this. He has no recollection of an act of ordinary goodness, but Agatha and Thomas remember it as if it happened yesterday. So many years later an act of kindness Ian had forgotten lives on in them. He who was so keenly aware of his shortcomings had no inkling of the grace he had been for them. He who had focused so much on the death of his brother never realized what a source of life and goodness and love he had been for them. Agatha, Thomas, and Daphne knew that Ian had been living a forgiven and forgiving life — a truly gracious and redeemed life — even if he did not, and proof of it was what his love had made of them.

Earlier we reflected on how sometimes the consequences of our actions live on in ways we never expected or intended. We focused then on the consequences of our misdeeds and how they can damage and harm in ways we never imagined. But what the story of the "Hearts-of-Palm" dish suggests is that the same is true for the good things we do. The consequences of any act of kindness, any act of thoughtfulness, generosity, and love can change people's lives in ways we may never know. Who is to say that what we took as nothing more than an act of everyday goodness does not live on as a stimulus to goodness in another? For so long Ian has seen his life through the prism of a single mistake, but Agatha, Thomas, Daphne, Reverend Emmett, and all the members of the Church of the Second Chance see it quite differently. They see him as a man of abiding goodness, gospel innocence, and rare, resilient love.

The novel ends with Ian married to Rita the "Clutter Counselor," a woman who "makes her living sorting other people's households and putting them in order."[58] Rita and Ian have a son, Joshua, and in preparation for this gift of new life Ian the carpenter — now a true craftsman — makes a cradle for his son.

He who can make beautiful things with his hands has surely made something beautiful of his life. If becoming a Christian is like learning a craft, Ian Bedloe has surely mastered the craft of forgiveness, and the goodness and love which flow from it. No longer an apprentice, he has been born again on the other side of failure and become, if not a gospel virtuoso, at least a saint maybe.

In this final chapter we have explored how indispensable forgiveness is to any human life. None of us can survive without forgiving and being forgiven because forgiveness is the only power we have over the hurts, regrets, wounds, and misgivings we are not able to change. Freedom comes from forgiveness, hope too, but only because forgiveness redeems the hurts and errors that cannot be erased. Forgiveness brings life, but forgiveness does not always come easily, and that is why it is often an ongoing process that must be revisited and renewed. Perhaps most importantly, forgiveness is a gift — a grace — we are called to embrace and embody. For anyone wishing to reflect further on how we can heal the pains and sorrows of the past, on the nature and importance of forgiveness, on what happens when forgiveness is not offered or experienced, but also on whether forgiveness is always possible or advisable, the following may be helpful.

Hanson, Ron, *Attitus*
Hawthorne, Nathaniel, *The Scarlet Letter*
Hijuelos, Oscar, *Mr. Ives' Christmas*
Lomax, Eric, *The Railway Man*
Mason, Bobbie Ann, *In Country*
Morrison, Toni, *Beloved*
Prejean, Sr. Helen, *Dead Man Walking*
O'Neill, Eugene, *Long Day's Journey into Night*
Shakespeare, William, *Romeo and Juliet*
————, *The Merchant of Venice*
————, *The Tempest*
Steinbeck, John, *East of Eden*
Wiesenthal, Simon, *The Sunflower*

Notes

1. Doris Donnelly, *Learning to Forgive* (Nashville: Abingdon Press, 1979), from the introduction.

2. Anne Tyler, *Saint Maybe* (New York: Alfred A. Knopf, 1991). Subsequent page references to the novel refer to this a edition only. Different editions, of course, will have different page references.

3. Tyler, 5. **4.** Tyler, 33. **5.** Tyler, 44. **6.** Tyler, 45. **7.** Tyler, 46. **8.** Tyler, 46. **9.** Tyler, 47. **10.** Tyler, 73. **11.** Tyler, 53. **12.** Tyler, 60. **13.** Tyler, 60. **14.** Tyler, 61. **15.** Tyler, 63. **16.** Tyler, 81. **17.** Tyler, 82–83. **18.** Tyler, 83. **19.** Tyler, 85. **20.** Tyler, 100. **21.** Tyler, 90.

22. Jerome A. Miller, *The Way of Suffering: A Geography of Crisis* (Washington, D.C.: Georgetown University Press, 1988), 114. **23.** Ibid., 112–13.

24. Tyler, 116. **25.** Tyler, 116. **26.** Tyler, 116. **27.** Tyler, 117. **28.** Tyler, 116. **29.** Tyler, 116. **30.** Tyler, 119. **31.** Tyler, 122. **32.** Tyler, 122. **33.** Tyler, 122. **34.** Tyler, 122. **35.** Tyler, 122–23. **36.** Tyler, 123. **37.** Tyler, 123–24.

38. Dietrich Bonhoeffer, *Life Together,* trans. John W. Doberstein (San Francisco: Harper & Row, 1954), 111. **39.** Ibid.

40. Donnelly, *Learning to Forgive,* 66. **41.** Ibid., 66–67.

42. Bonhoeffer, *Life Together,* 110. **43.** Ibid., 112.

44. L. Gregory Jones, *Transformed Judgment: Toward a Trinitarian Account of the Moral Life* (Notre Dame, Ind.: University of Notre Dame Press, 1990), 82–83.

45. Bonhoeffer, *Life Together,* 23.

46. Donnelly, *Learning to Forgive,* 67.

47. Tyler, 127. **48.** Tyler, 127.

49. Jones, *Transformed Judgment,* 112–13. **50.** Ibid., 115.

51. Timothy F. Sedgwick, *Sacramental Ethics: Paschal Identity and the Christian Life* (Philadelphia: Fortress Press, 1987), 60.

52. Vincent Macnamara, *Love, Law and Christian Life: Basic Attitudes of Christian Morality* (Wilmington, Del.: Michael Glazier, 1988), 192.

53. Tyler, 201. **54.** Tyler, 224–25. **55.** Tyler, 260. **56.** Tyler, 305.

57. Donnelly, *Learning to Forgive,* 65.

58. Tyler, 285.

ACKNOWLEDGMENTS

There are always people to thank when writing a book. I am forever grateful to Germain Legere, C.P., Owen Duffield, and Gus Wilhelmy, three of my English professors in high school, who brought literature to life for me and awakened a love for reading. That passion was deepened by Dr. Tom Kemme, Dr. Wade Hall, and Dr. Kathy Lyons, all professors of English at Bellarmine College in Louisville. It was there, too, under the guidance of Dr. Patrick Reardon, that I first learned to read literature theologically. For the past several years I have been a professor of religious studies at St. Norbert College in De Pere, Wisconsin. I am indebted to Dr. Robert Boyer, Dr. John Neary, Dr. Stan Matyshak, and Dr. Ken Zahorski, all professors of English at the college, for the suggestions they made, listed at the end of each of the chapters, of other works of literature through which the various themes of the book could be explored.

Special thanks is due Roy M. Carlisle of The Crossroad Publishing Company. His insights and suggestions for improving the book proved immensely helpful. Too, his encouragement and enthusiasm for this project helped sustain my own.

Finally, as always, thanks to my wife, Carmella. There have been many blessings to my life, but none more graced than when her story was added to my own. Carmella has taught me that God, indeed, is in the details.

About the Author

Paul J. Wadell is associate professor of religious studies at St. Norbert College. He received his B.A. in English from Bellarmine College of Louisville, his M.A. and M. Div. in theology from Catholic Theological Union of Chicago, and his Ph.D. in theology from the University of Notre Dame. In addition to his interest in theology and literature, other areas of research include the ethics of Thomas Aquinas, the role of the virtues in the Christian life, the importance of friendship for one's moral and spiritual development, and the mission of the church in contemporary society. He has contributed chapters to several volumes of theology and ethics and written numerous articles for religious and theological journals. Dr. Wadell has given lectures and workshops throughout the United States, as well as in Canada, Japan, and Rome. In May 2002 he was awarded the Donald B. King Distinguished Scholar Award by St. Norbert College. He is the author of *Morality: A Course on Catholic Living; Becoming Friends: Worship, Justice, and the Practice of Christian Friendship; Friendship and Moral Life; The Primacy of Love: An Introduction to the Ethics of Thomas Aquinas;* and *Friends of God: Virtues and Gifts in Aquinas.* He is married and lives in De Pere, Wisconsin.

OTHER TITLES OF INTEREST

Msgr. Lorenzo Albacete
GOD AT THE RITZ
A Priest–Physicist Talks About Science, Sex, Politics, and Religion

"Lorenzo Albacete is one of a kind, and so is *God at the Ritz*. The book like the monsignor crackles with humor, warmth, and intellectual excitement. Reading it is like having a stay-up-all-night, jump-out-of-your-chair, have-another-double-espresso marathon conversation with one of the world's most swashbuckling talkers. Conversation, heck — this is a Papal bull session!"
— Hendrik Herzberg, *The New Yorker Magazine*

0-8245-1951-5, $19.95 hardcover

John E. Thiel
GOD, EVIL, AND INNOCENT SUFFERING
A Theological Reflection

In this timely book, John Thiel allows for the reality of innocent suffering while affirming God's opposition to evil, suffering, and death. Faithful to the tradition, Thiel challenges classical, modern, and postmodern accounts of God's relation to evil. In doing so, he offers the outlines of a systematic theology based on God's promise to destroy sin and death.

0-8245-1928-0, $19.95 paperback

Richard C. Sparks
CONTEMPORARY CHRISTIAN MORALITY
Real Questions, Candid Responses

One hundred honest, engaging answers to the most asked about moral questions, from a leading moral theologian. This pastorally oriented guide gives the viewpoints of Roman Catholic, Protestant, and Orthodox churches.

0-8245-1578-1, $13.95 paperback

herder & herder

OTHER TITLES OF INTEREST

Rowan A. Greer
CHRISTIAN HOPE AND CHRISTIAN LIFE
Raids on the Inarticulate

Voted "Book of the Year" by The Association of Theological Booksellers!

What is the destiny of the human soul in this life and the next? Dare we hope to "see God face to face," or will our vision of God remain forever filtered "through a glass, darkly"? In this remarkable volume, Rowan A. Greer turns to the New Testament, the church fathers, and later writers to throw light on their own visions of the human soul. He suggests that Augustine of Hippo and Gregory of Nyssa represent two distinct strands of Christian thinking that find expression later in writers such as John Donne and Jeremy Taylor. Greer, who has trained two generations of historians and theologians in the rich thought of the early church, has succeeded in writing a volume that is both full of original scholarly insight and, by virtue of his elegant writing, accessible to laypeople and non-specialists.

0-8245-1916-7, $24.95 paperback

Please support your local bookstore,
or call 1-800-707-0670 for Customer Service.

For a free catalog, write us at

THE CROSSROAD PUBLISHING COMPANY
481 Eighth Avenue, Suite 1550
New York, NY 10001

Visit our website at
www.crossroadpublishing.com

All prices subject to change

herder &
herder